W9-BSS-546

RESIST
THE
POWERS

— WITH —

Jacques
Ellul

RESIST
THE
POWERS

— WITH —

Jacques
Ellul

BY CHARLES RINGMA

PIÑON PRESS

P.O. Box 35007, Colorado Springs, Colorado 80935

OUR GUARANTEE TO YOU

We believe so strongly in the message of our books that we are making this quality guarantee to you. If for any reason you are disappointed with the content of this book, return the title page to us with your name and address and we will refund to you the list price of the book. To help us serve you better, please briefly describe why you were disappointed. Mail your refund request to: Piñon Press, P.O. Box 35002, Colorado Springs, CO 80935.

© 2000 by Charles Ringma
All rights reserved. No part of this publication may be reproduced in any form without written permission from Piñon Press, P. O. Box 35007, Colorado Springs, CO 80935.

ISBN 1-57683-225-2

Cover photo: Walter Hodges/Stone
Cover designer: Dan Jamison
Creative team: Darla Hightower, Heather Nordyke

This publication is designed to provide accurate and authoritative information in regard to the subject matter covered. It is sold with the understanding that the author and the publisher are not engaged in rendering legal, accounting, or other professional service. If legal advice or other expert assistance is required, the services of a competent professional person should be sought. *From a Declaration of Principles jointly adopted by a Committee of the American Bar Association and a Committee of Publishers.*

Ringma, Charles.
    Resist the powers with Jacques Ellul / by Charles Ringma.
      p. cm.
    Originally published: 1st ed. Sutherland, NSW, Australia;
Clarmont, CA: Albatross Books, 1995.
    Includes bibliographical references.
    ISBN 1-57683-225-2
      1. Meditations. 2. Christian life—Meditations 3. Devotional
calendars. 4. Ellul, Jacques. I. Title.

BV4832.2.R54 2000
242'.2—dc21

Printed in the United States of America

1 2 3 4 5 6 7 8 9 10 / 05 04 03 02 01 00

Contents

——— DEDICATION ———

Marina, Renay, Leighton, and Jodie:
kasambahay kong kaibigan

Preface

THIS MEDITATIONAL BOOK IS ONE OF A THREESOME. ONE, *Seize the Day*, features the writings of the German theologian and martyr, Dietrich Bonhoeffer. Another, *Dare to Journey*, is based on the thoughts of Henri Nouwen, one of the great Dutch-born contemporary writers on spirituality.

This book, while sharing some common features with the other two, is quite different. Jacques Ellul, unlike Bonhoeffer, is not a trained theologian, but a French professor of social institutions who, like Bonhoeffer, ardently grapples with the relevance of faith in our modern world. Unlike Henri Nouwen, Ellul's concern is not so much with the disciplines of the spiritual life, as with the implications of our faith for the kind of world we are shaping.

Jacques Ellul is not only a prophetic voice, but a writer who provides a penetrating analysis of the ills of modern Christendom and of our social and political institutions. In suggesting answers, Ellul invites us to a faith that resists the powers of our age, embraces a vision of the kingdom of God, and combines prayer with social transformation. As we contemplate our Christian task in the third millennium where faith and freedom on the one hand and technological prowess and control on the other will increasingly be pitted against each other, Ellul's work will be significantly informative.

My thanks are due to Karen McColm who skillfully typed my handscript and helped with most of the secretarial work in the preparation of the manuscript, and to Darla Hightower for this Piñon Press edition.

Finally, I am most grateful to faithful friends in Australia and newfound friends in the Philippines and Canada who have provided love, support, and encouragement.

—CHARLES RINGMA

Introduction

THE KIND OF FORMAT AND THE TYPE OF MEDITATIONAL writing used in this book seems to me to be particularly appropriate.

The format, I think, meets a current need. We live in busy times and we are preoccupied with action and productivity. Consequently, we find it difficult to make time for reflection and prayer. This format, by virtue of its compactness, while not excusing our busyness, allows us to spend some time each day in prayer and meditation.

Why this type of meditational writing? And why use a profound scholar such as Jacques Ellul for a meditational reader? A partial answer is that the nature of meditational books needs to change. They are frequently too sentimental and lack theological content. They tend to be otherworldly and do little to help us focus our prayers on the things that daily occupy us in the real world.

A further answer is that only scholars tend to read Jacques Ellul. Yet there is so much he has to say that is pertinent to all of us. I have attempted, therefore, to make Ellul more readily available to the general reader.

As this format does not allow for a systematic presentation of Jacques Ellul's views, does it trivialize his thought? This yearly reader is no substitute for reading Ellul himself, but it will provide the reader with a sense of Ellul's thought. Similarly, this meditational reader is no substitute for reading the Bible. It serves, however, as a small footbridge into Scripture and into the writings of an important Christian thinker.

Ellul's thought is central to this book. But I have made no attempt merely to restate Ellul's ideas. That would be repetitive. Instead, I have entered into a creative dialogue with this great French Protestant thinker. Thus, two voices speak in this book, Ellul's and my own. In this difficult juggling act, I have in no way sought to muffle my own voice or elevate Ellul's. I hope that readers will be informed and inspired by this creative dialogue.

I trust that this book will serve you in its primary focus of seeking to bring head, heart, and hand together. Spirituality cannot be conceived apart from theology. Theology, on the other hand, need not be formal, academic, and arid. And spirituality is always practical in that it seeks to express God's love in our world of turmoil and strife.

The content of these pages is for thoughtful, reflective, and prayerful reading. I trust that the thoughts in this book will lead to a fuller appreciation of the faithfulness of God, of our prayerful dependence on His grace, and of our great calling to be light and salt in our dark world.

Introducing Jacques Ellul

WHILE I HAVE VAGUE MEMORIES OF COMING ACROSS the name of Jacques Ellul during my seminary days in the mid 1960s, it wasn't until 1975 that I seriously read his work, *Hope in Time of Abandonment* (1973). It was the title that had attracted me, for by that time many of the counterculture youth movements with which we were involved had run out of steam. Disillusionment had set in and many of us were trying to regain our bearings and sense of direction. Ellul's book was a beacon of light. While it acknowledged the silence of God in human affairs, it celebrated the power of hope, which keeps the future open.

In the following years, I opened and reopened Ellul's *The Ethics of Freedom* (1976), but my busyness prevented a careful reading. The reading of Ellul, I kept telling myself, will have to wait for another day.

It wasn't until the mid 1980s, after reading Ellul's *The Subversion of Christianity* (1986), that the further reading of Ellul became imperative. This was for a number of reasons. First, I had come to a point in my life where I needed to make sense of a decade and a half of zealously working for one cause or another. While much was accomplished, there had also been many disappointments. And, more pressingly, well-conceived plans and projects had turned out quite differently than expected. I needed answers and it was not difficult to see that Ellul's writing grappled with these kinds of issues.

Second, my own study pursuits had led to looking

more extensively at how sociology and theology affect each other. This made the reading of Ellul much more pressing, seeing that he had written extensively in both areas.

Having read over these past years most of what Ellul has written, how do I introduce him? Why have I written a meditational reader that incorporates some of Ellul's key thoughts? And, more importantly, how can I encourage my readers to take the plunge and read Ellul for themselves?

It is difficult to typify Ellul. He has written several books on the Bible: *The Judgment of Jonah* (1971), *The Politics of God and the Politics of Man* (1972), *Apocalypse: The Book of Revelation* (1977), and *Reason for Being: A Meditation on Ecclesiastes* (1990). But he is not a biblical scholar and these books are not traditional commentaries. They are much more idiosyncratic interactions between Ellul as a key thinker of our time and the biblical text. His books, therefore, are pregnant with contemporary meaning.

The rest of Ellul's writings fall into two broad categories: the sociological and the theological. In the former category are such books as *The Technological Society* (1964), *Autopsy of Revolution* (1971), *Propaganda: The Formation of Men's Attitudes* (1973), *The Betrayal of the West* (1978), and *The Technological Bluff* (1990). In the theological category belong books such as *The Presence of the Kingdom* (1967), *Prayer and Modern Man* (1973), *The New Demons* (1975), *Living Faith: Belief and Doubt in a Perilous World* (1983), *Money & Power* (1984), and *The Subversion of Christianity* (1986).

However, Ellul's sociological books are not traditional

sociology. They are more a philosophical reflection on key societal trends and issues. Similarly, his theological writings are not traditional theology. They are an intense treatment of particular themes rather than a broad-based systematic discussion.

At the heart of Ellul's sociological writings is his concern about the impact of modern technology on life and its shaping of human consciousness and structures. Here lurks in the author's mind the fear of the loss of human freedom and the specter of self-determination.

Ellul's theological writings celebrate the Barthian emphasis on the sovereignty and transcendence of God. Ellul argues for a vision of the kingdom of God rather than a mere preoccupation with the church, and proposes a Christian realism that combines prayer and political concern, faith and action.

The best place to start with reading this complex and gifted writer is his *Perspectives on Our Age* (1981) and *In Season Out of Season,* (1982). Both books summarize Ellul's key thoughts and provide some biographical detail. A third introductory book is his *What I Believe* (1989), which restates many of his important and sometimes controversial perspectives.

An early theological work that set Ellul apart as a significant thinker was his *The Presence of the Kingdom* (1967). Ever since, he has been the subject of debate. Some regard him as a writer with great prophetic insight into the issues of our time, particularly in his analysis of the role of technology in the modern world. Others see him as being too pessimistic, particularly in his work *The Meaning of the City* (1970). Others again see Ellul as essentially iconoclastic, particularly in his views of the church. They believe that he is far too critical of the church and not constructive enough. Others question the theological soundness of his ideas on "universal" salvation.

Ellul is marked by controversy. One major reason is that he defies normal categories. He is both a sociological and theological thinker, having been the professor of the History and Sociology of Institutions in the Faculty of Law and Economic Sciences at the University of Bordeaux, while at the same time being a leading Reformed churchperson. But he is not only a thinker; he is also an activist, having been deputy mayor of Bordeaux and also having worked ceaselessly on behalf of troubled young people and drug addicts. He owes much to both his Christian faith and Marxism, acknowledging both the transforming power of Christ in his life and the value that the writings of Karl Marx brought to his understanding of the social world. Yet he is certainly not a Marxist and he is not traditionally Reformed either.

A second reason for people's difficulty with Ellul is that his writings range over such a wide terrain and he makes no attempt to bring this diversity into a cohesive system. His writings include technology, law, politics, ethics, urban anthropology, theology, and the Bible.

A third and possibly the major reason that Ellul's writings have stirred such debate is that he writes with passion. He is not the calm, well-reasoned scholastic. He writes critically, incisively. He writes in order to incite.

So is Ellul worth reading?

The answer is a definite Yes if it is important to the reader to engage one of the leading Christian intellectuals of our time, to interact with a man who has his feet in both the world and the church, and to be open to being challenged by Ellul's critique of contemporary society and his castigation of many of the practices of the church.

The answer is likely to be No if the reader is insecure and defensive about his or her faith, doesn't want to confront the big issues in our world, has a pietistic and world-denying form of Christianity, and is not interested in a faith that is intellectually defensible.

But whether one comes to Ellul with a positive or a negative attitude, one cannot but be stimulated. Ellul is a controversial writer. He is never dull. His passion comes out of his willingness to squarely face the issues of life. Faith is not escapism, but a strident engagement. Hope is not a Utopian dream, but prayer and work that God's kingdom will continue to break into the rigid institutions and uniformities that we create.

And while Ellul can be incisively critical, he is never negative. He passionately believes that Christ has made the radical difference in our world and that God continues in history to engage us with His demands of discipleship and obedience. We can therefore take comfort that Ellul has not only deeply thought about God's kingdom project within our fallen world, with its powers of ideology and seduction that both mesmerize and confuse, but he has also attempted to "walk his talk."

There is little doubt that one of Ellul's major themes is that we resist the powers of this age because Christ has displayed their folly and invites us instead to live the lifestyle He advocated.

I am confident that this meditational reader will challenge the mind, touch the heart, and mobilize the hand for concrete action.

JANUARY

Resistance

The courage to stand against the prevailing ethos of our era commits us not to a path of narrow retreat, but to a search for positive alternatives.

Christians are the children of their era. They, like others, imbibe the values of their age. They also absorb this world's preoccupations and are drawn into its concerns. More specifically, Christians can, like others, be mesmerized by what the world has to offer and be seduced into thinking that the world only gives without also taking. While the world of God's creation needs to be celebrated and our social world needs to be impregnated with spiritual values, the worldliness of the world needs to be resisted.

Jacques Ellul reminds us that "the first duty of free people is to say No."[1] Christians are called to stand against every form of evil and oppression in our world, but this can only occur when the evil in our own lives and in our religious institutions is acknowledged and we commit ourselves to the task of creating the new by first becoming renewed ourselves.

Action
Don't simply say No. Our No must lead to the Yes of working for real change.

Confession

If we start with changing ourselves before attempting to change others or our world, we may well affect others more deeply than if we had only preached at them.

We all find ourselves in circumstances or situations that we desperately want to change. And in grasping for solutions, we are quick to lay blame at the feet of others. *If only they hadn't done that, then I wouldn't be in this difficulty,* we readily rationalize to ourselves.

But problems are seldom the sole product of another's making. We, most frequently, also play a part. Sometimes, we only have ourselves to blame. It is the dawning realization that I may need to own my part of the problem that provides the first shaft of light. It is my confession that breaks the heavens open.

In the words of Ellul, "The moment when I say 'It is my fault' is the moment when the lancet of grace has pierced the abscess."[2]

Reflection

Acknowledging my wrong in relationship to others frees me from wrongly judging them and opens the door for reconciliation and peace.

Unmasking the Powers

*When the dominant ideas, values, and priorities
of a particular age are unquestionably accepted,
one may be in a greater prison than that made
of stones and iron bars.*

Some Christians are particularly good at sniffing out
all forms of personal evil. Many are less good at
identifying corporate evil. Many fail to see how the
national interest may disfavor the weak, how economic
policy may favor the strong, how our justice system
favors the rich, and how the social welfare system disempowers the poor.

While we need to take responsibility for personal
wrongdoing, we also must discern our part in supporting structures and causes that oppress others.
Jacques Ellul challenges us to unmask the powers of
our age. He writes: "People have always been possessed
by powers beyond their control. Yesterday, it was the
demons of the forest, nocturnal devils, phantoms
returning from the past. Today, it's money or politics
or technological excess."[3]

Reflection
*Refusing to be part of oppressive
structures will thrust us onto the
lonely road with Christ.*

Western Arrogance

*Our technological prowess has not achieved
more humane cities, a world of plenty, and
justice for all. Yet foolishly our faith remains
unshaken in what science may yet do, while
faith in the God who made us and calls us into
partnership remains so perilously fragile.*

One of the seductive ideas of the Western world is
that progress will inevitably lead to a better
world. But much of Western progress has been at someone else's expense. Much of modern Western history
is the story of exploitation. And exploitation has been
the convenient rationalization that has flowed from our
cultural arrogance.

Ellul points out that "the greatest fault of the West
since the seventeenth century has been precisely its
belief in its own unqualified superiority in all areas."[4]
Instead of encompassing the world in the footsteps of
the Suffering Servant, it subjugated the world in the tri-
umphant name of the "Christ" of Western imperialism.

While we cannot turn back the clock, we can
begin to join in genuine partnership with those in the
developing world.

Action
*While the colonial era is past, the West still finds
ways of exploiting the developing world. Let us
find ways to identify with those who are thus
treated and to champion the cause of the poor.*

Against Ideology

While Jesus calls us to freedom, we create
religious systems that frequently bind people.

Jesus was preoccupied with the kingdom of God and
the creation of a social movement that provided hope
for the marginalized and for all those who were
oppressed by the dogmatic religious systems of the time.
Jesus' concern was to bring freedom, reconciliation, healing, and peace. He empowered people to live a life of
faith, prayer, obedience, and loving service. He was not
preoccupied with creating a new religious system.

Sadly, we have been so preoccupied. And in creating our religious rituals, theologies, structures, and
programs, we have more frequently worked against the
intentions of the Man from Galilee than we have fur-
thered His dream. Thus we need the courage to
subvert our own rigid systems and overcome our own
ideologies.

In the words of Ellul, "We must attack all ideologies, since they force us to conform, join us to an
orthodox group, and sweep away our capacity for
choice and individual reflection."[5]

Reflection
The power to move beyond our best ideas
and our most efficient programs can only
come from the grace of Christ and the
enlightenment of the Spirit.

Beguiled

*The quest for truth is always difficult,
particularly because we are so easily
mesmerized by what is offered to us on
seemingly good authority.*

Jacques Ellul writes: "I realise man is terribly mal-
leable, uncertain of himself, ready to accept and to
follow many suggestions, and is tossed about by all the
winds of doctrine."[6]

This is so because truth is no longer our natural
possession. Instead, we walk the road of acceptabil-
ity and convenience more readily than the royal road
of truth. And since truth always comes with its
demands as well as its promises, we frequently find
truth an embarrassment, for it calls us to new accountability.

Thus, truth needs to be embraced. It needs to be
welcomed home. It needs to be accepted even against
ourselves. When it is welcomed in this way, it is no
longer truth because of some external authority, but
truth as the way by which we decide to live.

Reflection

*Truth comes to us in many ways,
including in the doing of those things
of which we are not initially sure.*

The Gift of Faith

Faith carries with it both great potential as well as great danger. Its virtue and power is to expect much of God. Its danger is to assume control over what God has so freely given.

Those who wish to change the world face the constant challenge also to change themselves. It is hard to know which is the more difficult. But what is clear is that those who are not working at changing themselves have no right to attempt to change the world. We don't need any more "saviors" who lack self-insight, self-awareness, humility, and a servant heart for the genuine welfare of others.

This, of course, is not to suggest that we should be perfect before we attempt anything. If that was the case, we would be condemned to immobility, for we seldom act out of a true faith and a true love.

Ellul concurs. "You know perfectly well that no faith is pure," but goes on to point us to the source of hope: "God is the one who sanctifies it."[7] And if God constantly purifies our lack of true faith and love, then the danger to assume control will be minimized. For we will recognize that the exercise of a great faith has not won the day, but faith in a most gracious God has.

Reflection
*God is the focus of our faith,
the purifier of our faith, and the
provider of faith's longings.*

Faithfulness

Many acts of obedience may not immediately change the world, but will unalterably change us and will affect those who come within our sphere of influence.

There is something frustratingly disarming about Jesus of Nazareth. He gives us a vision for building the new community, but calls us to faithfulness in small projects. He empowers us, but calls us to be servants. He calls us to global responsibility, but encourages us to work in our neighborhoods. Thus, while the big and grandiose constantly swim into view, the personal caring, giving, and loving is what is called for. Ellul makes the point that "the course of history belongs to God and if we as Christians have any influence on it, it is first of all by our faithfulness to his will."[8]

Doing the will of God will always present us with a greater challenge than doing our Christian ministry, building our Christian structures, and applying our Christian solutions to the problems of the world. For our Christian structures and solutions seldom reflect the radical compassion and genuine servanthood that characterized the life of the Man of Sorrows.

Action
Take the small steps of obedience necessary to do the Master's will. They far outweigh the plans we make to save and affect the world.

Alertness

*Those who grasp the opportunities when they
come, rather than those who plan for the right
circumstances, will win the day.*

While the Christian life can be awesome because
we must responsibly carry God's light and love
into our dark world, it is also refreshingly simple. For
since we can neither change the world by ourselves nor
spiritually transform one single individual, our task is
to grasp the opportunities that God gives. This means
that we must be open and flexible. More particularly,
it requires that we must be discerning, for God-given
opportunities often come in strange forms and guises.

Jacques Ellul reminds us that "even apparently
insignificant things in life may be vital, and that means
we must be on the alert."[9] One step taken in obedience
to God's small promptings but unknown design may
have far-reaching consequences. Jean Vanier could
hardly have known that his simple response to several
persons with a disability could have led to the establishment of L'Arche communities around the world.
Those who dream of power and significance in God's
kingdom will be denied. Those who respond to the small
opportunities will be given greater stewardship.

Action

*At appropriate times, follow the
whispers of the heart rather than
the rationalizations of the mind.*

Partnership

*God frequently links His sovereignty and
power to our responsibility and obedience.*

Our work in the world for reconciliation, justice,
and peace can never be done apart from God's participation. By ourselves, we cannot achieve any of these
things. However, God's work in the world, though by
no means limited to our involvement, frequently
invites our cooperation. Ellul notes that God "associates man with himself in his acts and in the execution
of his work."[10]

This partnership between God and ourselves is
never a predictable alliance. For God sometimes
chooses the most unlikely people. And sometimes the
smallest and even unintentional actions most perfectly
fit into God's design. Thus, while God invites us into
a partnership with Himself, our part will always
remain the surprise. Our part is more likely to be the
evidence of God's grace than the result of our own cleverness and maturity.

Reflection
*Partnership with God is always
a privilege. It is not something we
can control and manage.*

There Is No Terminus

*When we have had our most profound
spiritual experience, the God of the
experience beckons us forward.*

We are quick in building our shrines and equally fast in turning spiritual experiences into strategies and programs. We feel safe with our religious systems and love the God of our predictable ceremonies. Ellul notes that "through laziness or enthusiasm, we try to stop at the same spiritual experience."[11]

But God, while consistent in His faithfulness and love, cannot be contained within our religious systems. In fact, He frequently seeks to subvert them and calls us forward to new adventures of faith and service. God is more the One who journeys in the tabernacle than the One who resides in the temple. As a consequence, a creative restlessness should characterize our walk of faith rather than a predictable compliance to ceremonies that bring security and certainty, but may leave us trailing behind the God who is ahead of us.

Reflection
*When we think we have learned enough in our
spiritual walk, we have stopped walking and
may well have ceased to be spiritual.*

A Practical Faith

*Spirituality joins faith and doing, prayer
and practical care, worship and concern
for our world.*

Jacques Ellul notes that "Christianity has progressively become a disembodied spiritualism."[12] Much of contemporary Christianity has not only become inward and introspective, but this inwardness has more to do with self-development than with a passion to find God in the still place.

Moreover, much of Christianity is still characterized by retreat from the evil world rather than an engagement that seeks to transform the unjust structures of our world and penetrate the fabric of society with the gospel as salt and leaven. Such a practical faith that concerns itself with the economics, politics, art, and culture of our time is a faith that will need to be deeply rooted in faith, prayer, and worship. For unless it is a faith that catches a glimpse of the kingdom of God and its justice and mercy, it will have little to say to our age.

Reflection
*The inward journey to the place of solitude
need not be a retreat, but can be an
empowerment for engagement
with our broken world.*

The Beguiler

*If evil was always visible in blatant form, most
men and women would readily reject it. But
because evil frequently comes in subtle form, it
is embraced before it is recognized.*

There is nothing virtuous about maintaining a
naive belief that in time things will get better. An
optimistic belief in progress fails to see that progress
is mainly the gain of some at the cost of the many. A
more biblical view is that true progress involves justice for all and this can only occur when evil is
overcome. The purging of evil is not only a personal
matter. It also involves overcoming evil in all its institutional forms.

The difficulty here is that these very institutional
realities sustain our life in the world. Thus we need
to become critical of the very systems that give order
to our society. We find this difficult, for we simply take
for granted so much of our social world. To the extent
that we do this, we underscore Ellul's observation that
the "devil has veiled his face."[13] For the areas of life
where we take things for granted are the very places
where the beguiler can do his work unhindered.

Reflection
*The Devil's most subtle work usually
occurs in those areas of life that we
fail to question critically.*

Individual Care and Corporate Concern

In building our many institutions of care, we may well be caring more for ourselves than for those the institutions are meant to serve.

In seeking to express God's concern and care for our world, we have majored on making institutional responses. The hospices of the ancient world, the youth refuges, and the old people's retirement villages of the modern world are but a few examples. While many of these institutions may do much good, they can tempt us to believe that the majority of us can leave the caring to the expert few.

Ellul is skeptical of expert solutions and institutional responses. He writes: "God never proposes that people collectively should turn society into an earthly paradise, [but] only that individuals called to very specific tasks fulfil his purposes."[14] Indeed, if the many rather than the few would practice hospitality and care, many of our institutions would not be necessary.

Action
Find your true calling in being Christ's servant to others, whatever your vocation and profession might be.

In the Arena

In both our personal actions and our corporate
responsibilities, we are called to display the values
of the Son of Man who reminds us that an inner
purity cannot result in social irresponsibility.

We live out our beliefs before a watching world. Ellul reminds us that "we must not deceive ourselves: the eyes of all men are fixed on us."[15] What people are looking for is not always self-evident. They may not be looking for the Messiah. But they are looking for a consistency between our words and our deeds. Thus, we are in the arena under the spotlight, not because people are seeking the light, but because we who claim to live in the light often do so poorly.

Instead of resenting the gaze of others, we should be grateful. For their scrutiny calls us to greater consistency and, in their appraisal, they may yet see a glimmer that resonates in their being. Thus in our attempt to save ourselves and to save the name of Christ from further contempt, we may inadvertently lance the darkness in another's life.

Reflection

While we may not impress many by our acts
of faith and care, we should offend no one by
the way we live a life of discipleship.

Being and Doing

Spirituality is an intimate rhythm between retreat and engagement, between reflection and practical action.

A spirituality that focuses only on self-development, personal reflection, and quietude is a distortion of Christian discipleship. A spirituality that only knows struggle, work, and giving, on the other hand, will not sustain itself. When brought together, they form a rhythm of the spiritual life where faith joins work, prayer results in action, and solitude fuels service.

While Ellul is right in his assertion that "being has to express itself in doing,"[16] he is not suggesting that doing is all that should legitimately characterize us. There is more to the human person than worker, actor in history, and producer. Even though God has placed us as vice-regents in His world, requiring our stewardship and care, He also calls us to worship and prayer.

Reflection
Beneficial work will always be born out of prayer and sustained by intercession. On the other hand, such work will always call us to prayer, for its achievement will have more to do with grace than with our cleverness.

Economic Justice

*Whereas our economic systems tend to condemn
the poor to perpetual dependence, God's economic
justice allows for the possibility to start again
with a clean slate.*

Much of what characterizes Western capitalism is
to gain advantage over the other without concern
for the consequences that may have on the other. The
idea of taking without concern regarding the cost on
others has already backfired environmentally. We
can't keep on exploiting nature without nature taking
its own revenge. Similarly, we can't keep on exploiting poorer nations without negative consequences
rebounding on our own heads.

God's justice operates on the logic that those who
always take will eventually be empty-handed, while
those who give and seek to bring reconciliation and
equity will also be blessed. Ellul, in recognizing this principle, writes: "We [in the West] have no choice but to
regard ourselves as debtors to the rest of the world. We
owe back what our ancestors took."[17] Justice is therefore always equitable, but also full of mercy and grace.

Reflection
*When our spirituality can also express itself
in economic justice, it demonstrates
how costly faith really is.*

For Others

*The blessing of receiving is that it makes
us candidates for generosity.*

The person who has come to faith in Jesus Christ,
who has had sin's stains removed and has been
endued with the Spirit, is rich indeed. The poverty of
a life without a transcendent center point, without faith
and hope, without the removal of guilt, and without
the Spirit's empowerment is a difficult life indeed.

The richness of the life in Christ, however, does
not mean that all our problems are solved, all our
wants are met, all our dreams are fulfilled, and all our
pain is alleviated. Being in Christ does not mean that
we live in Utopia. For with Christ we are to live in the
real world with all its contradictions and possibilities.
And with Christ we are to be in the world as servants.

Jacques Ellul reminds us that "from the moment
faith develops in us, we must be permeated by the conviction that, if grace is conferred on us, it is primarily
for others."[18]

Thus, the life that we have in Christ is a life that
participates in the anguish and needs of others.

Action
*Serve others even though such service
sometimes painfully cuts across your own
priorities and needs. When it is done
out of love for Christ and your
neighbor, it usually enriches.*

God's Secret

*In the wisdom of God, there is much that has
been revealed, but some things remain hidden.
That which is hidden is knowledge we would
like to possess, but is information we would
probably abuse.*

The walk of faith is marked by joy and struggle. Our
prayers are both persistent and negligent. Our
vision is both strong and faltering. And our service in
the world is on the one hand sacrificial and beneficial,
and on the other selfish and unproductive. We thus
live between the polarities of success and failure.

Since failure and difficulty are not due simply to
structural factors but also to the sin in our own hearts, we
can easily become weary in the struggle of life and in our
task to serve God in the world. While obedience rather
than success should keep us going, the greater motivation
to faithfulness is that finally it will be God Himself who
brings in the rule of love, peace, and righteousness. When
that day comes, "the Word of God will break over man
and declare: 'Lo, the trial is over.'" This moment, Ellul
notes, "is God's secret."[19] Thus, while we work for God's
kingdom, He alone will bring it to fulfillment.

Reflection

*There is an intimate connection between our
role and God's task. We will never unravel
how much is ours and how much is God's. But
we should pray as if everything depends on
God and work as if everything depends on us.*

The Fragility of Faith

Faith's power and certainty does not lie in the strength and persistence of our belief, but in the faithfulness of God.

Ellul makes the confession: "I know deep down that what I believe is uncertain, fragile, unstable . . . and at the same time I know existentially that this belief is a vital necessity for me, that it's the vital centre of my life."[20] This statement reflects what we all frequently experience. While we experience faith's certainty, we are also plagued by doubts.

Yet even in our doubting, we are kept by God's hand. For rather than turning away, we may question our motivations, search our hearts, press God for answers, and struggle toward the light. Embarking on the struggle of faith demonstrates how essential faith is to our lives. For if we still seek faith when it appears to produce nothing, then we give it an immensely high value. We seldom retain something that causes us so much difficulty and anguish of heart. When we do, however, then its importance cannot be exaggerated.

Reflection

In the dark night of the soul as well as in the time of faith's boldness and power, it is God who sustains us.

The Prophetic Word

While a prophetic word can be awesome in its challenge, it also brings a message of hope and deliverance.

The contemporary church clearly favors the "priest" to the "prophet." While the former works centrally to maintain the system, the latter is at the periphery calling for change and renewal. As such, prophets are the great disturbers, while priests are the healers and comforters. Although the church needs both, it has usually marginalized the prophet. His or her voice is only listened to in times of crisis.

This is most unfortunate, for much of the prophet's role is not so much to solve crises, but to prevent them. Ellul notes that "prophecy is the exact opposite of all ideology."[21] What he means by this is that the prophetic word can modify the religious system, practice, and theology before it becomes rigid, one-sided, and authoritarian. Thus the prophet is not needed when it is obvious that we have made a mess of things.

The prophetic word is needed as the discerner of early wrong trends and developments.

Reflection
If priests are in any way similar to the bureaucrats who keep the system going, then prophets are the change agents to whom we urgently need to listen, for they are open to a new future.

Activity

Activity is not enough. It must have the welfare of others in view more than our own dreams of what may benefit them.

The Christians who once defined the Christian task in the narrowest of terms—preaching the gospel— have rediscovered that proclamation and practical service belong together. As a result, they have embarked on a wide range of development projects, particularly in the Third World. Much of this activity is under careful review. For the task is not simply to put new projects into operation, but to make sure they achieve appropriate outcomes.

This is the challenge in all practical service. What we think may be best for someone else may not be what he or she perceives to be his or her need. We must learn to listen before we act.

Ellul rightly condemns the "absurd activism which plunges blindly ahead, bringing about results just the opposite of what it intends."[22] This implies that all activism must also be discerning and must submit to the searchlight of evaluation.

Action
Apart from those times when there is a need to respond spontaneously to someone's need, we should provide long-term help by a careful strategy that has in view the self-development of others.

A Little Good

While many small deeds of kindness can make a significant difference, these can also reinforce a system that cries out for transformation.

In situations where maintenance is required, continual deeds of love and service will have the salutary effect of improving the quality of life. Much of life is concerned with maintenance. Relationships, marriages, work environments, social groups, Christian community, and organizations and institutions all require nurture, sustenance, and care.

However, in the important task of caring for what we have, we must not become blind to what needs to be changed. Ellul warns that "we must be on guard lest love simply adds an innocuous good to a world which is a little bad, but which we have to humanise and make a better place to live in."[23] Since genuine care involves doing what is best and just, it is by its very nature transformative. Genuine care will always work for the greater good of all, not simply for the convenience of some.

Reflection
To maintain relationships, while at the same time attempting to improve and to transform one's social reality, requires detachment, love, and great courage.

A Dynamic Relationship

The joy of relationship is maintained by new acts of openness, availability, kindness, and care.

Jacques Ellul reminds us that "our relation to God is not a mere repetition, a fixed thing, a ritual, an exact submission, but a permanent invention, a new creation on both sides."[24] While word and being should never be separated, our relationship with God is more than a creedal confession. It is also a relationship of love and trust. As such, it is open to an ebb and flow.

Such a relationship can deteriorate. It can also grow. And, as we change, gain different experiences of life, and are pressed by new issues and concerns, we discover that God has journeyed with us. He is the God of childhood faith, of youthful activist faith, of questioning faith, and of a faith that has finally come to peace. God is the One who nurtures and cares as Mother and directs and guides as Father. God heals and wounds. He empowers, but also withdraws. Thus, while our creedal confession may remain the same, our experience of God is never static.

Reflection
If a relationship is static,
it is deteriorating.

Reductionism

In the final analysis one cannot live by slogans,
but only by a wisdom born of life experience.

Christians seem to be adept at sloganeering and much preaching is slick and simplistic. Formulas are given for receiving guidance, success, or healing. The varied nature of Christian discipleship is reduced to certain priorities and techniques. And the richness of Christian tradition and thought is emasculated by denominational formulations. Jacques Ellul laments "the reduction of the complexity of the message [of the gospel] to a single theme."[25]

Christian thought is far too rich for such treatment. For God is both the wholly other and the One who draws close in the Incarnation. This world is both created and sustained by God's power and yet is under sin's sway. We belong wholly to Christ through faith and yet are called to be in the world as light, salt, and leaven.

Reductionism unsuccessfully tries to overcome the polarities in which the Christian must live. It therefore makes the disturbing good news of the New Testament a good news that fits our cultural expectations. In doing this, it robs the gospel of its power.

Reflection
Since life itself is complex, a simplistic
gospel will soon become irrelevant.

Humility

*The greater our spiritual experiences, the more
we recognize how little we know of God's ways.*

While some people have an almost innate and
unspectacular experience of God's work in
their lives, others testify to dramatic events. Some
speak of a powerful conversion from a life of degradation. Others have been wonderfully healed. Some
have been used by God to bring hope to others, while
others have experienced significant dreams and
visions. There is no doubt that God works in many and
varying ways His wonders to perform. And whether
these wonders are unobtrusive or dramatic, they are
nonetheless miracles of His grace.

Those who experience the quiet working of God
must not despise its significance. Those who experience the dramatic working of God must not become
proud. Ellul rightly reminds us that the person "filled
with the Holy Spirit knows only a small part of the
mysteries and even of the action of God."[26]

Reflection
*We all experience God differently.
Rather than comparing our experience
with that of others, we should celebrate with
thankfulness and humility the specific
ways God works in our lives.*

Freedom and Responsibility

Freedom needs the sober reminder of responsibility lest it becomes anarchic. Responsibility needs to be infused with freedom lest it becomes legalistic.

Christians live between polarities. They don't only belong to this earth. They also belong to the world to come when God's kingdom is consummated. Similarly, they are truly justified in Christ and free from guilt and shame. Yet they are also sinners in need of forgiveness and reconciliation. Living between two polarities is most significantly illustrated in the tension between freedom and responsibility.

Christ has set His followers free from the Law they could not keep and which could never justify them, and yet He calls them to fulfill a higher righteousness. He frees them from sin's curse, calling them not to live for themselves, but to do His will and purpose.

The call of Christ to use freedom responsibly does not lessen the reality of that freedom. It only magnifies the importance of the choices Christians need to make now that they have been set free. Ellul rightly points out that "God grants man freedom to do other than God expects."[27] Such is the reality of the freedom we now have. But at the same time, God will always challenge us to do His will.

Action
Test in real life whether the responsible use of our freedom does in fact lead to further freedom.

Hope

*Hope is not inactivity. It is the strenuous
reordering of one's inner self in anticipation
for the things to come.*

To claim that we have become a generation of prag-
matists is almost an understatement. We are
characterized by a restless urge to do more, and productivity is the focus of much of our lives. It is equally
true that we aren't particularly good at inner reflection
and prayer, for our restless urge to achieve penetrates
even the sanctuary of solitude.

If we were to become persons of hope, however,
then both our feeble attempts at prayer and our fever-
ish activity to achieve would be revolutionized. "The
person of hope," Ellul asserts, "is the person who
waits."[28] Such waiting is never inactivity or passive resignation. It is a strong knowing that something better
must occur in our personal and social world. It is
accompanied by an equally strong sense that we of ourselves cannot bring about the greater good.

But it also involves a readying of ourselves for the
part God may call us to play. Thus hope curbs our restless activity by setting our sights on a greater good and
truer achievement. And it focuses our prayer on the God
who must intervene and prepare us to play our part.

Reflection
*Hope will change the things we do if we have
our sights on the God who is ahead of us
and who calls us to truer achievement.*

Love's Bias

Love's bias is that it sees the other person with the eyes of faith, seeks the other's welfare, and makes protective room for the other's self-development.

Jacques Ellul makes the observation that, while we can't be objective about the person we love, "we know the beloved as nobody else can."[29] Love has a way of seeing much when others see little. It goes on believing when others doubt. It gives when others have long ago given up.

There is nothing very rational about love, for love has its own explanations. There is nothing very predictable about love, for love knows its own seasons. There is nothing very calculating about love, for love knows its own generosity. And love cannot be quantified, because it is reckless in its ability to give.

While there is more to understanding the nature of love, the pressing issue for our world is not just more understanding. It is the practice of the art of loving. Such a practice can only come from those who, having been loved, can express love. For the experience of love has made them into loving persons.

Reflection
*While another's deeds of love shape our
very being, our own acts of love
continue to shape us as well.*

The Cry of the Poor

Judgment Day will be full of surprises. Those who have done much will expect to be amply rewarded. But they already have their reward if their deeds of kindness were not done "to the least of these brothers and sisters of mine."

The plight of the poor is not only that they are destitute. They are also oppressed and exploited. Moreover, the poor have internalized the reality of their social world. They are therefore characterized by hopelessness, fatalism, and despair. Ellul points out that "Christianity should have taken up the cause of the poor," but instead "it has served as a prop of the powerful."[30]

This generalization on church history seems to be a lesson that we are in the process of repeating. The great church renewal movements of the last decades of the second millennium have not benefited the poor. Instead, they have given more to those who already have much. Yet God's heart is with the poor even while our footsteps have turned the other way. As a consequence, our conversion has been incomplete, for we have embraced the benefits of the grace of God rather than the Father's heartbeat. Thus we have not truly come home. We are still wayward sons and daughters.

Action
Embrace the Father's concerns for our world even though this involves the most radical reorientation of our lives.

The Macro Issues

*Good people can create evil and oppressive
structures.*

We have become aware that evil does not only lie
in the hearts of men and women. It also lies in
the fallen nature of our world. And the doing of evil is
expressed not only at a personal level; it is also
expressed through the unjust and oppressive structures
that we have created. Not only do many of our institutional services favor the already favored, but we always
seem to find money to build new opera houses while
leaving our mental institutions in disarray and disrepair.

Jacques Ellul reminds us that "individual attitudes
cannot solve general problems."[31] What he means by this
is that we need to take responsibility not only for our
personal values, but also for the structures we support
and create. Being kind while serving in an oppressive
structure does not negate the negative impact of such
an institution. Put more sharply, the idea of being a caring person in the employ of Hitler's gas chambers is a
morally repugnant notion. We have therefore a responsibility for a life of inner purity, which is expressed in
supporting social structures that promote justice.

Reflection
*As Victor Hugo has so powerfully pointed out
in his Les Misérables, it is "the galleys that
make the galley-slave" and not only the lack
of moral fortitude of the individual.*

FEBRUARY

Prayer and Necessity

Prayer is the heartbeat of the spiritual person.
It ought to become as natural as breathing.

Made in God's image, we are attracted naturally to commune with the Creator. As like is drawn to like, so we find it normal to share our life and journey with the God who walks our common journey. Sadly, this idyllic picture of a relaxed fellowship as a parent with a child has become deeply disturbed. Driven by a deeply embedded guilt because we have not given God His rightful place in our lives, we find this relationship has become marred. Moreover, we have lost this childlike innocence. We seem to be more in flight than in fellowship. We seem to struggle more with God than enjoy His presence.

The impulse for prayer has therefore to take a new turn. It is no longer a sharing of two parties who are quietly at peace. Prayer now is the cry for reconciliation. It is frequently the cry for mercy. Jacques Ellul reminds us that "if the need to pray is not present, then all the models and procedures are useless."[1] But the need to pray is ever with us for, without the cry for God's grace, we are lost.

Reflection
If prayer is the luxury that we can afford
only when we are in some personal
crisis, then it is not prayer.

No Explanation

*We have every right to question God. He
has every right to answer as He sees fit.*

Our relationship with God is dynamic and changing.
There are times when this relationship is trusting
and peaceful. At other times, it is doubting and tumul-
tuous. Sometimes we go through a questioning phase.
So much in this refractory world does not seem to make
sense and things we had hoped for do not work out.

But God welcomes the questioning person. He
invites us to come, not only with our sin and pain, but
also with our concerns and questions. In fact, it is
always better to come with our questions rather than
to brood and sulk and, finally, withdraw. This, however, is not to suggest that God will always provide
answers for everything that we want to know.

Jacques Ellul reminds us that "God does not
explain his conduct and decision to man when the latter demands an account."² Much of what God does will
remain inscrutable to human understanding. But He
will respond to us and lovingly work with us until we
have come to peace.

Reflection
*Questions that come from uncertainty
and pain, rather than those that come
from bitterness and anger, will
always receive an answer.*

Listening

*The modern person is not without his or her
religious questions. While these questions may
not be framed in church language, they are
questions requiring a discerning response.*

Jacques Ellul suggests that "we must learn what the
question is which is really being asked by the person
of this age."[3] This requires a radical reorientation by many
of us who are Christians. We are generally not good at
listening, for we believe that we have the answers for our
era. Consequently, proclamation rather than careful discernment is what characterizes us.

But a further reorientation is required. It is not
enough to become listeners so that we can then proceed
with giving our answers. Careful listening requires that
we move beyond our ecclesiastical fortresses and our
defensive postures. It involves joining with others in their
hopes, pain, and ideas as well as in their questions. In
such joining, we will not only come closer to the real
questions, but we will discover that some of our answers
will need to be modified.

Answers formulated in the safety of the community of faith may not be as relevant as those forged in
the midst of daily life.

Reflection
*In listening to the questions of this age,
we can more relevantly discern
God's will for this time.*

The Long Search

*Even after the initial search to come to faith
has ended, we will continue to search for
fulfillment and peace.*

Augustine's dictum that our hearts are restless
until we find our rest in God is true. Restlessness
is an especially good depiction of the person without
faith. And Ellul deepens this description with the
observation that "the seed of man's questing is to be
found in Cain's life in the land of wandering, always
searching for a place where his need for security might
be satisfied."[4]

What is not true, however, is that all our searching comes to an end once we have come to faith in the
God revealed in Jesus Christ. The search continues. In
fact, it intensifies. Having found a new center point in
Christ, we embark on the long search to discover the
implications of our faith for all of life. Moreover, we
discover that we need to accept Christ more fully, drink
more deeply of His Spirit, and discover more of His
truth for our lives and for the world.

In the long search of discovering all that Christ
would have us to be, we often feel that we have only
begun the journey.

Reflection
*Those who think they have arrived
have not even begun the journey.*

Truly Radical

The truly radical element in early Christianity was its community life that resulted in economic sharing.

Jesus formed a community of disciples. They shared a common life as well as a common mission. This discipleship community based on servanthood became a model for the communities of early Christianity. While some would argue that the vision of the Jerusalem community was a Utopian ideal, the house churches of the Pauline Gentile mission were equally concerned with practical sharing and caring.

Sadly, much of contemporary church life knows little of this community model. Other models that cater more to our Western individualism have become prominent. Ellul, however, rightly points out that "Christians . . . should be militant . . . they have been called to make up a living, active community based on fraternity."[5] The building of base communities is nothing less than a radical act. It demonstrates that Christ has called us into a fellowship where the needs of the community rather than our own needs become a primary concern and where the needs of the world become the focus for the community's action.

Action
Join with others in a common service to the world—this is potentially the most life-changing action we can take.

Playing Our Part

*Responding to others in the way that God
has so graciously responded to us provides
the dynamism for new life in a tired world.*

Ellul makes the assertion that the Christian "has a
part to play in this world which no-one else can
possibly fulfil."[6] Many would agree with this. But what
the Christian's contribution should be is variously
understood. Some have very grandiose ideas of the
Christian's role in society. They see the Christian as the
sole builder of the new society. Others are quite pessimistic. They see the Christian contributing little
besides an emphasis on morality and spirituality.

Both these extremes miss the point. Christians are
to be neither the saviors, nor the moral guardians of society. They are simply called to demonstrate in every
aspect of life the reality of God's love, justice, and mercy.
They are to show that grace triumphs over evil, that love
dispels hate, that forgiveness disempowers anger, and
that justice and mercy overcome exploitation.

Moreover, they are to be signposts to the fact that
God is building a kingdom in which we all may joyfully participate.

Reflection

*It is simply not true that Christianity does not
work for the betterment of this world. It is true
that Christianity has not always been a force for
love and justice because those who profess that
faith have not always lived up to their own ideals.*

The Will of God

*The call of God usually ruffles the even
flow and pattern of our existence.*

There is a sense in which the will of God should
become part of our everyday existence. In the normal rhythm of daily life, we should live according to
the values of God's kingdom. In living according to
God's Word, we do the will of God.

But God also has a way of calling us to do specific tasks. As Ellul observes, "When God addresses a
man, he does not merely give singularity to the man;
he also particularises his will for him."[7]

It is this specific calling that disturbs the even pattern of our existence. It frequently involves doing
something that we had not anticipated. It most certainly
involves the rearrangement of our priorities. While it
may not necessarily be difficult, it does require a flexibility on our part and a willingness to do even that
which does not make a lot of sense to us at the time.

But sometimes this particular will of God is most
demanding. When this is the case, we can only cry out
that God's grace and enabling will sustain us.

Action
*Do the specific will of God, not as an aberration
in the rhythm of your life, but out of a
heartfelt desire and expectation.*

Until the End

*The transformation of society remains a
continuous possibility in the partnership
between God and us.*

There are times when new social movements bring
new hope to our repressive world. There are also
periods when the church as a transforming community breathes new life into decadent structures. New
ideas have permeated society for the better and new
economic conditions have brought benefits for large
numbers of people.

But every change movement has also brought with
it new problems, and change has usually been followed
by new repressive forces. There is no smooth, upward
process to a better world. There are only times of opportunity when women and men seize the day, or times
when we squander the impulses for justice and peace.

For since God continues to be providentially
involved in our world, working redemptively in human
affairs, change for the good is always a possibility. As
Ellul notes, "History will not end until every possibility of combination between human initiative and
divine initiative is exhausted."[8]

Action
*While change for the better is always
a possibility, grasp with both hands
the most opportune time.*

Living the Impossible Dream

There is nothing finally achievable about living the Christian life. It is always beyond us, yet it is our present possession.

Jacques Ellul is adamant that "what the New Testament really means by being a Christian is the very opposite of what is natural to us."[9] He could not be more correct. The Christian life is the attempt to live the impossible dream. This is not to suggest that we don't have a firm relationship with Christ through faith. Nor does it suggest that we cannot be sure about the life to come as we continue to live in Christ by the Spirit.

What it does mean is that living the lifestyle of the kingdom of God will cut across all our normal values. For in God's kingdom, the least are favored; the great are to become servants; those who have all are impoverished; those who are the social outcasts are welcomed home; the blind are made to see; and those in bondage experience release. This is a new order of which we naturally know little. But Christ invites us to enter this new world, promising to train us and to remain with us as our encourager and supporter.

Action
*Love and practice servanthood. In that
action, many of our ethical dilemmas
as to how we should live and respond
to others are dissolved.*

Empty Hands

*Prayer is not the art of exchange where I give
to God what I think He wants in order to get
what I think I need.*

Prayer is not the art of exchange. Nor is prayer the
art of bargaining. Rather, prayer is the art of vulnerability. It is the recognition of our creatureliness and
the acknowledgment of God's greatness, love, and
mercy. It is the confession of our powerlessness and our
need for God's intervention and protection. It is the
acknowledgment of our waywardness and wrongdoing,
and seeks God's grace, forgiveness, and empowerment.

These are never exchanges. We don't hand to God
our sin and He automatically hands to us forgiveness.
For God's grace is out of all proportion to what we give
to Him. God's forgiveness is always a miracle. It is a
free and undeserved gift. Prayer as the art of vulnerability, therefore, recognizes that we come to God
empty-handed.

Ellul emphasizes this and adds a timely warning.
He writes: "We seek to fill our hands with things which
we bring in order to hide the fact that we are not bringing our lives and ourselves."[10]

Reflection
*Our nature is always to prefer bargaining
to vulnerability. God's grace, however,
seeks to make us more vulnerable.*

Those Little Acts

While we weigh the social value of our actions,
God weighs the motivations of all we do.

In every age, Christians have had different understandings regarding what was the best way to relate
to and to serve society. Some emphasized prayer.
Others promoted charity. At certain times, the priority was education and agricultural reform. In our day,
it is evangelism coupled with social concern.

We need to be careful, however, that we do not
reduce our Christian response to the world to single
programs. And we must at all times avoid mere sloganeering. For God calls us to many acts of love and
care—to promote justice rather than to achieve specific programs.

Ellul emphasizes that "I have to realise that the
acts I think [are] indifferent might be the very ones
that God retains."[11] Our programs and God's will may
well overlap, but they are seldom the same. For when
we major on work, God might well call us to prayer.
When we emphasize justice, God may well call us to
do mercy.

Action
Respond to God's will through the
leading of the Holy Spirit and so
remain relevant and flexible.

All Is in Question

*Our certainties are at best fragile. For
when God reveals Himself in His power
and greatness, we are speechless.*

It is inevitable that we build our religious structures
and dogmas. These provide continuity and support
and, at their best, will provide some sustenance for our
journey of faith. The danger is that we might ultimately
depend on them. For our hope should finally be centered on God alone. God has a way of facilitating this.
There are times when we are shaken loose from our
structures and certainties.

Ellul comments on his own experience: "All was
called into question and I found myself once again
before the unpredictable plan of God."[12] Such an experience can fill us with dread and uncertainty. It can call
the very basis of our faith into question. And it can
darken our future, for we cannot see the answers that
lie on the other side of the abyss.

At such a time, we need to discover that God is
not only the God of our previous certainties, but also
the God of the abyss who will carry us across—providing we can entrust ourselves fully to Him.

Reflection
*When all is shaken loose, new
realities can appear in their place.*

Building the Kingdom

The kingdom of God is both a creative and destructive force. It creates the new, which usually in time will need to be replaced because we have made it rigid, legalistic, and idolatrous.

Jacques Ellul is very concerned about the end result of our strategies to better the world. While he insists that we must preach "good news" and promote God's order and justice in our world, he warns that "one error consists in believing that by constant progress in this 'order,' we shall attain the kingdom of God."[13]

The second error that compounds the first is that we will then institutionalize our achievements and so preserve the progress that we think we have made. All such attempts have not had a good track record. For structures can hardly contain the kingdom of God and, even while they may temporarily embody something of the kingdom, this soon becomes tainted by legalism.

The kingdom of God is more likely to subvert our structures than to support them. But the subversion is never a negative process. It is positive in that it creates new possibilities.

Reflection
It is a great blessing that we cannot create and maintain the kingdom of God.

Abundant Life

The life that God gives is always more than
what we deserve and can rightfully expect.

While life itself has its particular mysteries, life's journey is even more full of surprises. This statement assumes that we haven't reduced life to the predictable and have begun to live mechanistically, governed either by our fears or insecurities. Some people have tried to make life so safe that they have squeezed out every bit of adventure. Others have attempted to be so much in control that they have imprisoned themselves.

God's gift of life, on the other hand, has nothing to do with predictability and control. Instead, it throws us into the adventure of life with God's Spirit ever leading us onward. This kind of life has nothing to do with immobility and safety, but with risk and abandonment to the will of God, which draws us into the unknown and the previously unimagined.

Sadly, many contemporary Christians have not understood the radical freedom that God's gift of life has given them. They only ever see God as fortress and never as the Great Leader ahead of His people. They are afraid of life rather than being drawn into its challenges or possibilities.

They fit Ellul's pertinent description: "The less you live, the more you read about other people."[14]

Reflection
Abundant life always
involves faith and risk.

The New Birth

The new birth starts the journey of faith and
obedience. It is never the terminus.

Many churches in the Western world are full of people who have come to faith through the easy gospel. This gospel proclaims happiness, but fails to speak about obedience. It celebrates joy, but fails to speak of struggle. It speaks of faith, but not of costly service. This gospel accents what God will do for us, but fails to develop how our relationship with Christ draws us into God's concern for a world of righteousness, justice, and peace.

The easy gospel can quickly lead to disillusionment, for faith in Christ does not mean that all our problems are instantly solved and we live happily ever after.

Ellul rightly emphasizes that the opposite takes place. "The new birth leaves us with our difficulties and adds new problems."[15] That new problems should arise is inevitable. Faith in Christ turns our life around. It is hardly surprising that this has all sorts of repercussions. And that old problems don't immediately disappear has nothing to do with the weakness of God's power. Instead, it has everything to do with the way God has chosen to transform us.

Rather than miracle solutions without our involvement, God has chosen to change us at the pace that we respond to Him in faith, humility, and obedience.

Reflection
The new life in Christ is as
much warfare as it is peace.

Nothing Is Lost

*With the eye of faith, blessing and difficulty are
both seen in the light of God's providential care.*

Life cannot be compartmentalized. The effects of our
worship on Sunday are likely to spill over into the
rest of our week. And the realities of daily life are likely
to intrude into our Sunday worship. The blessing of
solitude is likely to mingle with the cacophony of our
workaday world. And the issues of the workplace are
likely to become topics for prayer and reflection. Not
only can spirituality not be divided from daily life, but
all of life can be experienced as characterized by God's
involvement.

Ellul notes that "nothing in human relationships
lacks meaning: neither a chance meeting nor an illness
that attacks us."[16] This does not mean that God is
mechanically manipulating everything that happens to
us. Since we have been given the gift of freedom and
responsibility, life is much more open than that. But it
does mean that nothing needs to be lost. It means that
in the seemingly random events—the times of great
joy and the periods of darkness or difficulty—God is
accompanying us with His grace and benediction.

Reflection
*The God of the Cross and of the Resurrection
knows how to enter into all the key
experiences of our lives, including the
painful and the seemingly senseless.*

The Way of Powerlessness

The power of moral influence is frequently more powerful than the power of position, because the latter is so easily corrupted.

We all need to face the question regarding appropriate uses of power. For we all exercise power in some way and are subject to the way that others exercise power over us. While some believe that all power is necessarily coercive, others distinguish between inappropriate and appropriate uses of power. Clearly, the use of power exercised to enhance the well-being of the other person is a beneficial use of power. While personal use of power is one thing, institutional exercise of power is something else again.

Jacques Ellul is adamant that the church should not seek political power in an attempt to bless the world. He writes: "When Satan offers to give him all the kingdoms of earth, Jesus refuses—but the church accepts, not realising from whom it is receiving the kingdoms."[17] The church, like Jesus, should walk the way of powerlessness. This way involves obedience to God and the way of servanthood, rather than the use of positional power, which can so easily become self-seeking.

Reflection
To resist the use of power, which so frequently benefits ourselves, is to overcome a great temptation.

Prayer and Hope

Prayer always looks forward to what God may yet do. As such, it is a key that opens up new possibilities.

Sometimes, prayer is the last resort. We begin to pray when we have exhausted every human possibility. Prayer in these circumstances usually takes on a frantic and demanding tone. If only we had begun to pray earlier! Prayer should occur at the very genesis of a project, not simply when failure stares us in the face.

Ellul underscores this perception. He writes: "Prayer is the assurance of the possibility of God's intervention, without which there is no hope."[18] Without God's intervention, there is no possibility of ultimate success. And because God's intervention is required at all times, prayer becomes a continual necessity, not only for the big decisions and the major projects, but for everything—even for life itself, which we so frequently take for granted.

Because prayer looks to God to do what we cannot, it is always bathed in the hope of new possibilities.

Action
*Pray in order to live,
not simply to serve.*

The City

*The city promises much. But it seldom
achieves community and justice.*

There is little point in pining for a Garden of Eden or
longing for a return to a preindustrial primitivism.
The die of modernity has been cast. The city came up
"heads." And it has become such an all-pervasive reality
that the "country" no longer forms a contrast to the city:
It has become subservient to the insatiable demands of
the city.

Ellul has been quick to point out that the city is
more than a sociological reality. Moreover, the city is
never simply neutral. It is a place of power and influence.
He writes: "The city has . . . a spiritual influence. It is
capable of directing and changing a man's spiritual life."[19]

It does this not only through the crippling power
of its broken promises where the hoped-for economic
progress dissolves into the ever-growing numbers of
the poor and where the dream of community is shat-
tered by alienation and isolation. It also does this by
the power of its seductive images that suggest permanence, solidarity, and security.

Action
*Work to establish God's subversive
kingdom of community, justice, grace,
and vulnerability in the midst of the city.*

A Critique of Capitalism

Capitalism has produced great benefits and has spun great delusions. Its seductive power lies in its inability to produce a society based on justice and fraternity.

There is a certain unfairness in criticizing the hand that feeds you or the system that sustains you. On the other hand, an economic system that may be reasonably good can develop all sorts of serious aberrations. Ellul critically looks at modern capitalism. He thinks that it subordinates the person to money and thus "making money becomes the purpose of life."[20]

These values are a far cry from the gospel, which celebrates life rather than possessions. The gospel is critical of much-having and encourages stewardship and generosity. More strongly, the gospel sees wealth as the great temptation that overpowers people and prevents them from enjoying a messianic lifestyle. Such a lifestyle sees God as the provider and imitates God's generosity toward us as the way we are to serve others.

Action
*Declare enough is enough and be willing
to relinquish that which has power
over you, so that you can begin
to walk the road of true freedom.*

A Secret Work

Many Christians are quietly working in the
corridors of power as well as in the slums of
degradation. Many more seek to express their
faith in Christ in their homes, neighborhoods,
and workplaces. All are like a secret force that
seeks to infiltrate the worldliness of the world
in order to bring the light of Christ.

Christians are part of the world. But they hold dif-
ferent values. They love peace rather than violence.
They are concerned about people rather than systems.
They promote reconciliation rather than division. They
build community rather than encourage individualism.
They encourage forgiveness rather than retaliation.

More than that, while Christians build the world,
they place their hope in the world to come. They seek
to effect societal change, but look to God as the liberator of all things.

Christians fit uncomfortably into the world's systems, programs, and ideologies. Their vision of life
transcends contemporary values and their hopes and
dreams are never fully aligned with the social and political forces of the day. Ellul makes the comment that,
like a spy, the Christian is "to work in secret, at the
heart of the world, for his Lord."[21] While Christians
may not always do brilliantly, a life of faithfulness will
have its desired effect.

Action
Work in such a way so that no part of the
world and its systems are left untouched
by the grace and love of God.

The Common Good

The divisions between good and evil are not so easily drawn. The children of the light can do much harm, while the children of darkness can do much good.

Someone has made the comment that the problem with Christianity is that it has never been tried properly. There is an element of truth in this, because we all imperfectly reflect the life and love of Christ. We tend to water down the radical demands of the gospel and so we easily substitute the rigidity of the law for the freeing power of God's grace. As a consequence, the problem of evil lies also within the church.

At the same time, the world, marked by God's common grace, is not wholly devoid of good. Frequently, nonChristians demonstrate great fairness, initiative, and care. Ellul makes the point that even "the very people who are so evil have a fundamental thirst for good."[22] The thirst for good is especially with those who recognize their sinfulness. It is seldom with those who are self-righteous. More particularly, this is frequently true of those whose lives are broken by alienation, despair, or life-controlling problems.

Reflection
God draws near to the brokenhearted and accompanies those who seek to do justly, whether they are Christians or not. However, He resists the proud and self-righteous, Christian and nonChristian alike.

Change

*Change can only occur when new possibilities
are envisaged and embraced.*

Personal change does not occur easily. We seem to
hold onto the old and familiar, even when that may
be hurting us. Thus, pressure or difficulty of itself is
usually not sufficient to bring about lasting change.
Something more is needed. Ellul speaks of the "changing of man in the presence of God's promise."[23] In this,
he points to the power of the new that draws us forward into new ways of being and acting.

Because God's promise is never an empty word
but can accomplish what it envisages, it is a power that
sustains us in the journey toward the promised goal.
So the key to the change process is being empowered
to move forward.

Because the Holy Spirit is the One called to our
side, we can gain hope in the midst of doubt, strength
when we are weak, courage when we are fearful, and
perseverance when we feel like giving up.

Action
*While change may have its genesis when
we are dislocated or vulnerable, depend on a
vision of the new and on God's power to
sustain you on the way in order to progress.*

Never Enough

*Because we have lost the Garden of Eden,
we seek to find what lies beyond our grasp.*

We are characterized by a restlessness that either propels us to truer achievement or reduces us to a permanent state of dissatisfaction. Ellul believes that many people in the Western world are plagued with the latter problem. He writes: "The easier their work gets, the more they complain of deadly tedium. The more reasons they have to play and enjoy themselves, the more they get bored and go off in search of some inexpressible novelty."[24]

This indicates that the search for a purposeful life remains elusive for many. And this is hardly surprising. For the symbols of happiness created by our consumer society hardly resonate with the themes of the gospel where servanthood takes priority over self-aggrandizement, where reconciliation is more important than self-promotion, and where relinquishment is more valuable than much-having.

Little wonder that, when the members of society pursue materialistic values and lose a holistic vision for life, they quickly become bored or frustrated. For since life is a responsibility structure requiring giving as well as receiving, those who only take will soon become satiated and immune to life's great calling: to love their neighbor as themselves.

Reflection
*Much-having fails to bring us
into the Promised Land.*

The Obedient Son of the Father

*Obedience rather than power is the
hallmark of spirituality.*

Jesus has the power of divinity. But He did not use
that kind of power. He laid it aside. Instead, He used
the power of servanthood and obedience.

Ellul notes that "Jesus' . . . eyes did not see ultra-
violet rays, nor did his ears hear subsonic sounds. But
his eyes saw the heart of man and his ears heard the
words of God and his mind pondered the scriptures."[25]
It was love that focused His insight. It was obedience
that determined His destiny.

We are invited to walk a similar road. Laying aside
the power of position and status, we can live by the
power of authenticity and integrity. Moved by compassion, we can respond to achieve God's good for
others. And imbued with God's Word, we can walk to
the sound of a drumbeat that is different from the
inchoate sounds of our world. None of this, however,
will give us the inside edge on other people. Nor will
it necessarily give us prestige and influence. It will, however, give us the benediction of the Father's "well done."

Action
*Obey in the spirit of faithfulness rather
than with the desire for success.*

Prayer: Giving, Not Getting

In the act of prayer we not only acknowledge
our need, but we seek God's will and purpose.

Prayer should not be the persuasive attempt to convince God of the things we need nor the attempt to badger God into accepting our ideas. Instead, prayer should first of all be the art of intimacy. It is the act of drawing close. It is the way in which we develop companionship with the God who calls us to draw near.

Ellul speaks of prayer being an "act of complete self-giving."[26] It is the way by which we open ourselves to both the love and the discernment of the Other. It is God's love that brings renewal, healing, and hope. It is God's discernment that brings correction and redirection. Both of these ministries require that we wholly give ourselves.

In receiving healing and renewal, we need to expose our faults and hurts. In receiving redirection, we need to embrace God's will and purpose for our lives. With a renewed self that seeks to do God's will, we can wholly give ourselves to service.

Reflection
Prayer is always a dangerous activity
because it is a drawing near to
the God who will change us.

Discernment

*The Christian is to be both contemporary
and radically different.*

There is no virtue in isolating ourselves from the world. This will not safeguard our spirituality. But it will certainly condemn us to irrelevance. There is also no virtue in being culturally "trendy" and accepting blindly the latest offering in the round of personal and social "cures." At the same time, there is no merit in being out of touch with the critical issues of our time. Ellul laments that Christians are usually "several steps behind."[27] Consequently, they seek to provide answers to questions that people are no longer asking.

Instead, the Christian is called to be both relevant and different. If we fail to be relevant, we cannot be heard. If we fail to be different, we have nothing to say. This calls us to both a critical immersion in the issues of the world of our day and in a withdrawal for the purposes of reflection, prayer, and discernment.

Reflection

*Discernment first of all calls us to draw close.
It furthermore calls us to withdraw. It
finally calls us to purposeful action.*

Making a Difference?

*Our creative impact on the world has been a
mixed affair. Sometimes the world has influenced
the church more than the church has influenced
society. At other times, the church's witness has
been heroic and significant.*

While those of us who are Christians are called to
be change agents in our world—to pray and to
work that this world will reflect more of God's mercy
and justice—our impact is frequently limited. Jacques
Ellul puts this more strongly. "On the one hand, it is
impossible for us to make this world less sinful; on the
other hand, it is impossible for us to accept it as it is."[28]

This reflection identifies both our limitation as
well as our responsibility. While we may be able to
improve certain aspects of social and economic life, we
cannot change the insidious persistence of evil. Only
God can do that. In spite of this fact, we are called to
be salt and light and to overcome evil with good.
Moreover, we are called to demonstrate within the
Christian community that a new way of life is possible—not only for those in Christ Jesus, but for all,
because by His death and resurrection He has made
open the way for all.

Action
*Pray and work with God's glory in view, so
that this world will become renewed.*

MARCH

Nothing to Add

*The wisdom of the sages may help us in
understanding and applying God's Word. But
they have nothing to add to God's wisdom
revealed in Jesus Christ.*

There is a profound simplicity in the good news
concerning Christ. As the forerunner of the new
humanity, He offers us peace with God and His life-
giving Spirit so that our lives can be characterized by
grace and forgiveness. The challenge for all of us, however, is how we can make this simple message
applicable to all of life. What implications does our
faith in Christ have for family life, business, the arts,
politics, and our attitude toward the environment?

To help us in this journey of discovery, we will need
the Christian theologian, ethicist, and economist. But
they can only help us in the area of application. In the
final analysis, they have nothing new to add. As Ellul
points out: "The greatest saint or mystic can say nothing of value unless it is based solely on God's word."[1]
This is no less true for the Christian economist and the
ethical thinker. In their desire for contemporary relevance, they will need to return to the wisdom of
Scripture, which calls us to a way of life where power
is weakness, leadership is servanthood, freedom is doing
God's will, and love is the motive for all we do.

Reflection
*Even the wise need to
hear God's wisdom.*

Where Two Worlds Meet

The Christian should neither withdraw from the world, nor be lost in the midst of the world. Instead, the Christian should bring the reign of God and the world into collision.

In one sense, the Christian has escaped the world, because he or she need no longer be subject to its values and dictates. In another sense, the Christian is very much responsible for the world. For in the midst of this world, the Christian is to proclaim good news and demonstrate a set of values that reflects something of God's reign.

The Christian thus finds himself or herself at the point where two worlds meet. Jacques Ellul points out that "in this preservation of the world, the Christian ought to place himself at the point of contact between two currents: the will of the Lord and the will of the world."[2] This is a difficult position to be in. And the Christian is the first to feel the tension. The secret, however, is not to resolve the tension, but to live with it. If we resolve the tension, we either become so heavenly minded that we are no earthly good or we become so worldly that our vision of faith becomes irrevocably blurred.

Action
Take the stand of love for God and compassion for the world even though it will usually gain little appreciation from church or world.

Lack of Justice

*To take advantage of others for self-gain is
intrinsic to our Western values. Yet finally this
is nothing but a legitimized form of oppression.*

The biblical call for justice excludes every form of
exploitation and oppression. It invites us not to
take from the other for self-gain, but to empower the
other for his or her benefit and well-being. Biblical justice is much more than fairness. It is even more than
generosity, because liberality can so easily leave others powerless and can create dependence.

Instead, God's kind of justice involves treating
others in the same way that God has treated us. God
is more than fair and generous. He picks us up from
the ash heap of life and gives us a new self and a new
hope. We are all candidates for God's justice, because
we have all experienced the opposite.

As Ellul points out: "In every respect, our society is unjust for both individuals and groups."[3] By
contrast, in every way God wishes to demonstrate His
justice to all and in this He elicits the cooperation of
those to whom He has shown His mercy and grace.

Action
*Be a person infused with new hope
in order to be a mirror for others
as to what God can do.*

A New Frame of Reference

*To live by the grace of God for the glory of God
gives life a whole new frame of reference.*

Ellul points out that for many people "there is no
frame of reference and this generates anxiety."[4]

With this observation, he is not referring simply
to the nonChristian. Some who have no faith have
adopted a particular ideology as the guiding star of their
life. Some Christians also lack an adequate framework.

Some have faith in tradition. They merely follow
in their family's footsteps. Their faith is neither personal nor normative.

Some have a Sunday faith. They merely practice
certain religious ceremonies, but their faith has no relevance for the whole of life. And some see faith only
as an insurance for a future life. It therefore has no
present transformative power.

But faith in Christ cannot be peripheral in this
way. Because all things are from Him, through Him,
and unto Him, Christ becomes the center point for the
whole of life. His grace transforms. His power renews.
His Word guides. His Spirit empowers. And no part
of life is absented from His influence.

Reflection

*If only Christians would live the Christian life
holistically, they would be more integrated and
provide a greater witness to the world.*

When There Is No Prophet

*In the desire to make the church safe, Christians
have eliminated the critic and the prophet. As a
consequence, the church is bland and irrelevant.*

We repeatedly find ourselves before two choices:
the safety of uniformity and the risk of change.
It need not surprise us that the latter continues to be
the less preferred option. We are, after all, insatiably
creatures of habit. As such, we also set limits to growth
and development. Ellul, on the other hand, prefers the
risk of change by adopting the challenge of opposites.
He writes: "A person engaged in no dialogue . . . a
church without heretics, a sole party with no rivals,
is enclosed within the permanent repetition of its own
image."[5]

Yet we fear facing the other, particularly when the
other is significantly different. We resent exposure and
we find it difficult to admit our need for change. In
overcoming our fears, we need to recognize that the
role of the true critic or prophet is not to destroy, but
to build up by opening up to us new possibilities.

Reflection
*With no one to confront or to challenge us,
life quickly takes on a dull uniformity.*

Between God and Us

In the mysterious interplay between divine ini-
tiative and human responsibility, there is the
clarity of God's call.

Even though God is the supreme Lord and we will always remain mere creatures, we are invited to partnership. God is committed to the strategy of cooperation. And, as Ellul notes, the Bible is full of "the relation between man's action and God's."[6]

This does not mean that these two activities become blurred. Man's activity cannot become God's action. We cannot do what only God must do. But in the art of cooperation, God can call us to do His will and purpose and can empower and sustain us in such a way that we approximate His intention.

Much of what we do is done with fumbling hands. None of it is ever perfect. Some is done in such a way that it requires our repentance. But God can take the little in our hands and turn it into much. He can use vessels of clay to hold His glory.

Reflection
The strategy is not that perfect people do
God's work, but that obedient people
fulfill God's purposes in the world.

Micro and Macro Issues

*Transformation is concerned with both personal
and structural change.*

It is easy to suggest simplistic solutions for people
who are in difficulty or distress. It is even easier to
make irrelevant value judgments regarding the poor.
Our depiction that the poor are lazy and can better
themselves if only they will do something for themselves is a caricature that is far off the mark.

Ellul's comment that "we must continue to crit-
icise those who try to solve personal problems while
refusing to look at their social context"[7] is well
placed. The poor are frequently exploited. They suf-
fer neglect. They lack opportunity. They are frequently
demoralized. The attempt to explain their situation
simply in terms of personal problems fails to identify
their need for friendship, empowerment, and opportunity. If training and opportunity are placed in the
hands of the poor, they will respond. But the yoke of
oppression, condemnation, neglect, and judgment will
need to be lifted.

Action

*Offer the gift of friendship in the struggle,
companionship along the way, and the
creation of a "free place" to try again and to
start anew. This will help to break the powers
that are arraigned against the poor.*

Overcoming Isolation

*Being alone for the purpose of finding a creative
solitude is productive. Being alone through
isolation or rejection is destructive.*

We are not only made for God. We are also made
for community and human solidarity. Ellul
notes, however, that "in a society in which everything
is done to establish relationships, man is living in solitude."[8] This can occur not only in our cities of
anonymity, but also in the Christian community.
Mutual relationships of love and support cannot be
artificially created and cannot be institutionally based.
Instead, such relationships are forged through
processes of mutual self-disclosure and joining in a
common life and faith journey.

Yet this growth involves caring for each other
beyond common ideology, programs, and projects. In
these common realities, friendship may initially be
found, but cannot be ultimately sustained; for, in the
end, friendship is more than the sharing of common
ideas and projects. It is a commitment to mutual love
and care, even when we hold different ideas and are
called to different priorities.

Action
*Engage in the joyful and painful
journey of community-building.*

The Church in Opposition

While the church can play an integrative and cohesive role in society, it is frequently called to play a transformative role.

The church finds it difficult to be in opposition. It prefers to be in a supportive and legitimizing role. It more readily is in collusion with the existing power structures than in opposition. It more frequently seeks the blessing of the state than calling the state into question. The church more readily blends into the texture of the social landscape and less readily expresses itself as a counter-community.

Jacques Ellul notes, however, that "the church in the spiritual and theological sense always contains a current that is hostile to political power."[9] This is because the church is premised on the life and ministry of Jesus Christ. Because Jesus rejected the road to power and walked the way of suffering servanthood, the church must take a similar journey. It follows that, while the church would like to see itself as being central to the machinations of a society, it should operate from the margins to call society to a different way of life.

Reflection
The church in seeking power
loses its true power.

Seize the Day

While life provides us with many opportunities,
sometimes opportunity knocks only once.

It is simply incorrect to picture the Christian life as an existence where we always need to be on red alert to grasp every opportunity, and if we fail others will lose out on the good news in Christ. This places the intolerable burden of another's salvation on our shoulders alone. This eliminates God's participation, who alone can enlighten a person for faith.

However, we do need to seize the day. Jacques Ellul believes that we "must act at every moment as if this moment were the last."[10] This places us in the framework of obedience, not that of compulsion. This calls us to responsibility, not legalism. This invites us to look to God to lead and guide us. It does not mean that we have to do it all. This suggests a whole life of serving God and not simply faithfulness in particular programs and projects. Finally, this reminds us of our frailty and humanity. We need to play our part, but soon we will be gone, while God's work in the world will continue.

Reflection

Seizing the day always has more to
do with integrity than success.

To God's Glory

To live for God is neither a denial of self, nor an escape from the world. It is the discovery of our true purpose.

Jacques Ellul reminds us that "the years allotted to us on earth can have no other possible meaning or orientation . . . [than] that all our life should be to God's glory and in his kingdom."[11] This is not necessarily a call to the religious life or a call to full-time clerical ministry. Nor is it necessarily an invitation to embark on the spiritual disciplines as if prayer or worship are the only way by which we can live to the glory of God. We can live to God's glory while engaged in the most secular pursuits and in the most humdrum of daily activities. Our lives can give glory to God in both palace and pantry, in church and supermarket.

To live to God's glory is not some hallowed existence. It is simply living by the grace and love of God to bring honor to God's name and to demonstrate something of His love and nature wherever we find ourselves. In bringing glory to God, we can only do what pleases Him and what reflects His concerns.

Action
Take up the challenge of making God central rather than peripheral to your life.

Conversion

*Our conversion will always be incomplete.
Therefore, we must grow not only in
sanctification, but in making our conversion
more complete.*

If God's redemption were dependent on our thorough conversion, then no one would be saved. Not only is our conversion incomplete, but we usually convert with very mixed motives. Ellul notes that "some people convert because they're afraid of death, because they're in terrible pain and looking for consolation, or simply going along with a trend."[12]

In our present religious climate, Ellul's last point is a key factor. Becoming a Christian is presented as a basket full of promises. One can take anything from peace to healing to joy to prosperity. This gospel of benefits has made conversion a very attractive proposition. It has also made conversion thoroughly self-interested. Conversion can never simply be focused on what we gain. It more particularly has to do with turning to God as the only right way to live, even if this costs us difficulty and rejection.

Action
*Make the conversion process more complete
not through acts of service, but by being
conformed more fully to Christ.*

Harmony

*When harmony is won at the cost of diversity,
it loses its essential character.*

Harmony is seldom a windfall. Instead, it is a real-ity that needs to be won in the face of great odds. Ellul rightly points out that "harmony is to be found when certain events come together, but above all it is to be made, created, invented and produced."[13] Because harmony has nothing to do with uniformity, it will always remain a fragile commodity that needs to be continually re-created. Essential to harmony is the all-embracing concept of wholeness.

Harmony has nothing to do with eliminating the difficult or the problematical. Instead, harmony's aim is to integrate and to utilize that which we might ini-tially be tempted to discard. In achieving harmony, we seek to bring together those elements that seem to be opposed to each other. Harmony, therefore, not only creates peace. It also brings about a richness of life, for it draws into our orbit that which we first thought was incompatible.

Reflection

*Harmony will not be achieved by the insecure
and those who are easily threatened. It is
created by those who are secure in the knowledge that they can learn from others.*

A Life-Giving Word

A word of hope, encouragement, or direction
spoken in love at the right time can be life-giving.

Many of us are driven. We must achieve. We must be productive. Our activities must be purposeful lest we fail in being faithful stewards of all that God has entrusted to us. While there is virtue in careful planning and purposeful activity, this can never be the whole story. Life also has its surprises and its unexpected opportunities. And our creative response to these may well constitute the most important things that we do.

Jacques Ellul, in speaking of the girl in Naaman's household, notes that "she has borne the word of God and this is the decisive event in her life."[14] In an unexpected moment, she grasped the opportunity and spoke a word of direction that was to change the life of her master. Similar opportunities also come our way, but only to those who are available to God's direction and who prayerfully ask God to lead and guide them. Those who rush by in the busyness of their purposeful activity will not have the eyes to see.

Action
Be open to God rather than giving
total attention to the execution of all we
think is important. This is the
royal road to fruitfulness.

Action

*Purposeful action involves the doer's ability to
see things from the perspective of the recipient.*

Most of us are outwardly focused. And we easily
find ourselves involved in all sorts of activity. For
some the motto is "the busier the better." This feeds
our sense of self so that we see ourselves as useful and
productive. But much activity can also be counter-
productive. It can make us self-satisfied. Rigid.
Compulsive. Also, it can leave us inwardly barren.
Dissatisfied. Discontented.

It is important, therefore, that activity should not
only be draining. It should also be nourishing. And for
this to occur, action must be meaningful. Ellul emphasizes that "action without meaning cannot bestow
meaning on anything."[15] Further, action without meaning is never self-sustaining. Put differently, action that
is capable of the long journey is action that is born out
of hope and is made concrete by the call of God.

Reflection
*Action that is born out of our own dreams
is never as sustainable as action that
expresses our obedience to God's will.*

The God Who Is Near

*In our quest to find God's answer regarding our
particular issues and concerns, we usually discover that some of our concerns need to be
refocused and redefined.*

While we need to confess God as wholly other, we
do wrong to see Him as distant. Unfortunately,
we have made the two synonymous. In trying to overcome an inappropriate familiarity, we have made God
both alien and unreachable. The miracle is that God
draws close in His otherness. This is the good news
of the Incarnation: so different, yet so close. As Ellul
points out, the implication for prayer is that it "is not
addressed to one who dwells at a distance, but is
addressed to one who comes very close."[16]

Prayer is, therefore, a communication with the
One who knows all about us. It is addressed to the One
who does not need to be convinced about our frailty
and our struggle. It is a sharing with the One who has
entered into our pain. It is speaking with the One who
is committed to liberation.

Reflection

*God's nearness does not dispel His otherness.
His otherness does not prevent Him from
a sympathetic understanding. His
loving understanding does not prevent
Him from initiating change.*

Christianity as Ideology

*Ideology attempts to weave a consistent picture
of reality that then becomes the basis for all our
thinking and action.*

Christianity has almost always displayed a need
to build systems and structures. It has not only
built powerful ecclesiastical institutions, but also all-
embracing theological systems. Its hunger for empire
building has been monumental. The rationale for this
is most intriguing. On the one hand, the church justifies its centralization of power by claiming that in this
way it can best serve the world. On the other hand, it
justifies its theological systems as mapping out a
vision of how the world should be and how life
should be lived. In both instances, the rationale is to
serve the world better.

The reality is that the church so frequently
serves itself. And the ideology propounded by the
church both binds and blinds. For we may well question what is at best a myth that centralized power
enhances servanthood. Experience would indicate that
the two ideas are in radical opposition. Ellul's lament
therefore needs to be heard: "Christianity can clearly
also become an ideology. In fact, it has become one,"[17]
for ideologies serve no one but themselves.

Reflection
*Obeying the person of Christ is more radically
significant than following the dictates
of our ecclesiastical creations.*

The Power of the Future

*It is one thing to see the outline of a better
future. It is another to begin to live it, even
though others are still mesmerized by the old.*

Ellul makes the point that a true prophet does not
simply proclaim the new. A prophet, he notes,
"already 'lives' the future."[18] In doing this, the prophet
embodies the word and marks it out for authenticity.
In other words, a prophet brings word and deed
together, and begins to demonstrate the new as a present reality. The future is thus made present as a sign
of hope, as a harbinger of good news, and as a promise of better things to come.

This does not mean that everything the future
holds will be embodied in this prophetic demonstration. It is often only a glimpse, a precursor, a foretaste.
It therefore must not point to itself, but to that which
is yet to come. Sadly, the embryonic new is frequently
formalized and institutionalized rather than being given
the room for further experimentation and growth.
Because we want to possess the new, we fail to see that
it is merely the signpost to something better.

Action
*Leave the new alone and
it will lead us farther.*

The Work of My Hands

While we may celebrate the work of our hands
as God's good gift, we should never depend on it.
For it is God alone who sustains us and He
ought to be the focus of our adoration.

We are so often preoccupied with the things we
do and make. For we are marked for achievement and have an innate urge to produce, to shape,
to make changes, and to fashion our world. This in
itself is good. God has called us to be vice-regents and
to care for His world. But our work can become all-
consuming. It can become idolatrous.

Thus, we need to be freed not from the responsibility of work, but from its domination. Ellul notes
that "the final aspect of liberation from self is liberation with regard to 'the work of my hands'"[19] What I
do and achieve cannot be the core of what I am. While
God calls me to partnership with Him in changing the
world, He first of all loves me for who I am. In fact,
He loves me in all my vulnerability and need. And it
is this acceptance that constitutes the central core of
who I am. I am an amazingly loved person by the God
of all grace and mercy, and as such I can confidently
live to fully please God in all that I do.

Reflection
While I may want to be known for what I do,
I am loved by God for who I am.

Reluctant Obedience

*We pray for God's will to be done in our lives,
but we often struggle with the things that God
asks of us.*

Our highest good is to live to God's glory. The key
to bringing honor to God's name is to do His will.
But doing the will of God is often such a struggle for
us. Not only do we have difficulty discerning God's
purposes for our lives, but we fear that what God asks
of us will be too demanding. We believe that He is loving in His grace, but burdensome in His will. Ellul
remarks that, when people become aware of God's call,
they "begin by refusing and fleeing."[20]

However, a radical refocus is in order. For God
is loving rather than demanding in the revelation of
His will. His will is good. It is the path to life. While
His will may cut across our priorities and concerns and
may well call us to reevaluate our life's preoccupations,
the experience of doing God's will is in the long run
never irksome. It brings with it a sense of direction and
joy. It has its own particular surprises. It has its own
sustenance and empowerment.

Action
*We can do God's will by practically
aligning ourselves with God's
concerns for our world.*

Responsible Love

Love is the art of giving by a person who knows how to receive.

Jacques Ellul, in speaking of various stages in the development of love, claims that "after passionate love must come responsible love."[21] It is possible, however, to de-emphasize the idea of stages and to replace it with a much more dynamic model. One could say that the love of passion should nevertheless be responsible, for it must not lose sight of the other as person. One could also say that responsible love, which expresses itself in the daily rhythm of care, sustenance, and protection, must not simply lapse into maintenance mode.

It must also maintain a creative impetus. In other words, the one dimension should inform the other. Responsibility must make room for passion and the former should guard the latter. Without passion, love may develop security, but it lacks dynamism. But true love can never be without responsibility, because it expresses appropriate care for the other. And because every form of true love seeks the well-being of the other, love never ceases to be responsible.

Action
*Love as a way to bless
the other person.*

Religion of the Powerful

While religion in the hands of the rich is often a tool for control, among the poor it is a source of hope and consolation.

Ellul believes that the church throughout its long history has made some terrible mistakes, some of which are still with us today. A major mistake, he notes, was the emergence of Constantianism, which sought "to win over to Christianity the rich, the powerful."[22] The problem, of course, lies not so much in the church's attempt to attract the rich and powerful, but rather in its attempt to attract them on their own terms. It virtually meant that they did not need to go through the narrow door for, after all (so the argument went), if the rich and powerful keep their resources and their positions, then they can best serve Christianity.

Subsequent church history, however, has put the lie to that idea. For in becoming the protectors and benefactors of Christianity, they also became its controllers. Eventually, they redefined it. There aren't two gateways to the life of faith. There is only one, and this leads to an identification with the Word, which became flesh and dwelt among us.

Reflection

Jesus shows that power must be relinquished in order that true empowerment may occur.

Work and Prayer

*Work must be born out of prayer and should be
sustained by prayer. But work is not prayer.*

Not only do we prefer work to prayer, but much of
our work is an escape from prayer. We are so
intent on doing that which we think is so important
that we hesitate to pray lest we are called to reevalu-
ation. Ellul, however, rightly argues for the separation
of work and prayer. "To work is precisely not to pray
[and it is] necessary to interrupt work in order to stand
for a while before the Lord."[23]

But this does not mean that work and prayer have
nothing to do with each other. Precisely the opposite
is the case. At work, the Christian expresses something
of God's call to care for the world. This calls for careful prayer. Not only should we seek God's blessing on
our work, but our work should be in response to God's
call on our lives. Our work becomes the sphere in which
we express God's concern for the world. In sustaining
the daily rhythm of that call, we need refreshment and
encouragement. This can come from the discipline of
prayer, which inspires us to faithfulness.

Reflection
*Purposeful prayer will
always lead to work.*

The Power of Forgiveness

The secret of life is to respond to the
divine impulse to forgive.

In whatever way we may wish to describe life, it is clear that it is neither fair nor just. It is precisely this fact that provides the context in which we may exercise the power of forgiveness. For not only do we need to experience the forgiveness of others when we do them wrong, but we also need to extend forgiveness to those who have harmed us. It is, therefore, not surprising that Ellul can exclaim: "What else could we build our life on, if not forgiveness?"[24]

Forgiveness is not an incidental facet of life. It is central. For in the experience of being forgiven and in the act of forgiving, we promote life's key dynamic. Because life is the aspiration for the good in spite of a divided self in the midst of a broken world, it is little wonder that forgiveness becomes a central element. For we fail to do all that we would want. Others fail to be to us all that they desire. And things in life have a way of turning out to be different from what we have expected. While solutions are not always possible and resolution may be difficult, forgiveness is always appropriate.

Action
Forgive and be free from bitterness
and free the other from guilt.

Discernment

We create idols when we build ideologies and
perform practices that are not built on freedom.

There are a number of negatives that characterize
human existence. The first is that we easily lapse
into forgetfulness and fail to remember why we are so
busily doing what preoccupies us. A second negative
is that we easily lose the central core of the meaning
of our existence and proceed to create all sorts of sub-
stitutes. And third, we readily become so dominated
by what concerns us that we fail to maintain a holistic perspective on life.

All three can have implications for idolatry. The
first negative makes an idol of a kind of activism that
has lost its goals. The second creates idols because it
fails to acknowledge the truth. And the third lacks any
kind of discernment regarding current preoccupations.
It is here that Ellul's question is pertinent. He asks: "Are
we so sure, when we serve idols, that we can see they
are idols?"[25] His presupposition is that we are frequently blind. And in the light of the analysis of some
of our negative characteristics, Ellul is more right than
wrong. We more readily create idols than we are prepared to acknowledge.

Reflection
If we are not wholly centered on God, we are
likely to create some idols of our own.

The Mark of the Institution

*Institutions take on a life of their own that
readily becomes self-serving.*

Jacques Ellul comments that "there is a certain logic
in the evolution of institutions which is easily dis-
cernible."[26] This means that institutions tend to
possess some common characteristics. While these
characteristics may be used for good, they can easily
be used for evil. Because most institutions are centrally
controlled, they are frequently resistant to change from
the periphery. Most institutions develop a particular
culture. They have a certain history, expectations, way
of doing things, and set of goals. These are sometimes
jealously guarded even when the stated goals are no
longer being achieved.

Moreover, institutions can develop a morality
that weakens personal responsibility and integrity.
Because no one in particular is responsible for what happens in the institution, values can be weakened.
Institutions, therefore, must be kept open to change and
be held accountable. Women and men of courage are
needed to keep institutions honest and to work for their
transformation.

Action
*Care for the institutions we work in
and make them accountable.*

Church and Power

*Unlike the Master who renounced earthly
power, the church sees itself as a participant in
the power game and usually fares badly.*

The church continues to believe that if it has
resources, power, and influence it will use these
solely for the good of others. It is not alone in believing this myth. Other institutions make similar claims.
But the church should know better. Jesus' repudiation
of power in the desert temptation shows that earthly
rulership is a tenuous blessing. The use of earthly
power may not only take the church away from its true
ministry, but can corrupt the church at its very core.

Ellul remarks: "The scandal is that the church
tries to use political power to ensure its own authority and to secure advantages."[27] The lesson of history
is that the church's use of political power has nothing
particularly virtuous about it. The church also suc-
cumbs to power's temptations. But where the church
has relinquished such forms of power and has adopted
the power of servanthood, its political relevance has
not been lessened, but heightened.

Action
*Make the spiritual power of the church
socially and politically relevant by
using it to serve the world and not
simply the Christian community.*

Against the Tide

*The Christian's vision of life cannot but be
different from that of others because it gains
its inspiration from the Man who gave for
others His life to make peace.*

Jacques Ellul insists that the Christian "is the citizen of another kingdom and it is thence that he derives his way of thinking, judging and feeling."[28] This means that the Christian swims against the tide. It means that the Christian displays a contrary set of values and has a different vision of life.

But this does not mean that the Christian is always in oppositional mode, for any culture and every society is marked by both God's common grace and the fallen powers that influence the development of institutional evil. Put much more simply, there is usually both good and evil in every society. The good the Christian is called to protect and to enhance. Put differently, Christians are to be in solidarity with all that leads to justice in a society. But they are to be against all that promotes unrighteousness in our world.

The outworking of this opposition should not be mere harping criticism or moral indignation. Instead, it should be the act of demonstrating goodness in an alienated world, displaying the dove in the face of aggression, and working for justice in an unjust world.

Action
*We can act differently in our world because
we have been embraced by God's love
and have received His forgiveness.*

Self-Control

*All purposeful activity needs to be sculpted
within the framework of a desire to empower
rather than to dominate.*

Made in God's image, we are called to shape and
adorn the world in which we live. This activity,
however, calls for great sensitivity and wisdom. For
empowered with an ability to dominate, we easily
resort to harmful exploitation. Ellul notes that "action
is simply an expression of the will to dominate . . . and
those who win seldom have the wisdom to impose limits on themselves."[29]

Yet all sorts of limits readily suggest themselves.
These have to do not only with the limitations of the
earth itself, but also with the use of appropriate means
to achieve goals defined by justice. The most important
limitation, however, should be self-imposed. For because
we so frequently fail to grasp the greater picture and fail
to see the negative unintended consequences of our
actions, we need to proceed with true humility and flexibility. Moreover, because our motives are often mixed,
we need to be self-critical and open to the feedback of
others. A final point is that, because we lack wisdom, our
life should be characterized by prayer.

Reflection
*A person lacking self-control can hardly
exercise power appropriately.*

The Journey

*While we may long for certainty, God invites
us to the journey of faith.*

Christianity is a long attempt to build all sorts of certainties on Scripture. These have not only been the certainties of faith, but of economic progress and political ideology as well. Particularly in the political realm, Christians have frequently imposed their own values on Scripture. The Bible has not been allowed to speak for itself and has been contracted for an alien purpose. For as Ellul points out, Scripture does not provide final solutions, particularly not in the area of economics or politics. Instead, it gets us "started on a journey and the only answer we can hope to find is the one we ourselves give by our lives as we proceed on that journey."[30]

This does not mean that Scripture is irrelevant for the social world and only provides answers for an interior spirituality. But what it does mean is that we cannot baptize every current political ideal because it is sugar-coated with a naive religiosity. In the costly journey of seeking justice in our world, we may well find ourselves to be opposed to the very economic or political idols that first attracted us.

Action
*Practice economic justice, even though
doing so may mean being out of step
with both the Right and the Left.*

Beyond Ourselves

*Inner transformation involves the undoing of the
shame and guilt of the past and embracing the
new life God offers us in Christ.*

As human beings, we are constantly struck by our
vulnerability and finiteness. We are also aware of
our lack of perfection and downright selfishness.
Moreover, in spite of having enough and frequently
more than enough, we remain dissatisfied. Our lives
somehow lack the purpose and meaning for which we
inwardly yearn.

While many solutions to our predicament are
offered, the answer does not lie in the mere inward
journey. The inward journey eventually loops around
so that we face the same issues again. Instead, we must
make another journey—that of transformation. Ellul
notes: "For man has definitive need only of one thing,
to be loved, which also means to be pardoned and lifted
above himself." [31]

This transformation of the self through the grace
and power of God does not make us perfect, immor-
tal, or rich. It makes us forgiven, with promise of
eternal life through Christ and of being cared for by
the God of compassion.

Reflection
*Living beyond what we normally are only
makes us the people God has meant us to be.*

APRIL

Our Contribution

We can make our greatest contribution to the world precisely because we are obediently following the call of Jesus Christ.

Christians are frequently pulled every which way. Their loyalty to the Christian community can isolate them from the world. Their involvement in the world can weaken their participation in the Christian community. Clearly, Christians belong to both the community of Christ and the wider human community. And their God-given responsibility is to both communities.

Because God's love is for the whole world and not simply for the Christian community, Christians should be community builders as well as church planters.

But Christians cannot build the human community on its own terms. Ellul notes: "The world chooses its own methods and draws up its own plan of action in order to solve its problems; and people often think that, if Christians are to help preserve the world, they ought to join in these movements."[1] While Christians can collaborate with all humane impulses in society, their greatest contribution lies in their truly being disciples of Christ. For in such a discipleship, they will express not only a spiritual, but also a social conversion. Christians will begin to live a lifestyle marked by servanthood, equality, and transformation.

Reflection
If we are the people of God, we will be radically changed and as such become change agents in the world.

Tailenders

Christians are seldom the pacesetters in our
world because they fail to engage the world on its
own terms due to the insecurities of their faith.

Christians do not want to be known as religious
fanatics. So they fail to be zealous. And because
a faltering and decadent socialism has captured the language of political radicalism, Christians do not want
to be known as revolutionaries. So they pride themselves on their conservatism.

Consequently, "Protestants now are a nice little flock
of well-behaved sheep, obedient and utterly tame, though
they often think of themselves as pacesetters,"[2] Ellul
emphasizes. The same could be said for other Christians.
The failure of many Christians in having a formative influence in our world is because they have recast the image
of Jesus and follow a Christ of their own making.

Jesus died as a radical and subversive. He was eliminated because He was a threat to the system. Many of us
have made Jesus into a pious victim who suffered unfortunate circumstances. As such, He becomes a conservative,
while in reality Jesus challenged religious legalism and the
oppression of the poor, living the arrival of the kingdom.
Those of us who bear His name can do no less.

Reflection
If anything should characterize Christians,
it should not be conservatism. For Christ
radically calls into question the
values of this world.

Transformation

*If transformation only involves a change in the
structures and not in our consciousness, then the
old is likely to be repeated.*

Christians are to be the change agents in society.
Transformed by the grace of Christ and captured
by the love of God, they now seek to bring God's quality of life to the world. Therefore, the Christian's task
is more than one of protest against the evils of the
world. This does not go far enough. As Ellul rightly
points out: "A mere protest against the old ways is not
enough to avoid being recaptured by the old ways."[3]

The worldliness of the world needs to be transformed. This can only occur when Christians have
developed more than just a critical attitude to the world.
It can happen when critique is matched by love and
when love is expressed in costly service. It takes place
when the vision for change is not based on mere reac-
tion, but on the changes God's grace has powerfully
worked in our lives and in our Christian communities.

A transformed Christian community begins the
task of wider transformation by being a signpost that
change is possible.

Action
*Have a vision for the new and embrace costly
servanthood so that change can take place.*

Mixed Motives

*If we still need convincing that we can only live
by the grace of God, then we simply need to
acknowledge that even our highest expressions
of spirituality spring from mixed motives.*

Ellul states the heart of the matter when he writes:
"Every conversion is interested. Who can dare to say
that his own life and death are of no concern to him?"[4]
In other words, when we turn to God in repentance, this
is never because we are simply grieving about the fact
that we have offended God's holiness. It is also because
our failure is bringing us discomfort and difficulty.

Similarly, when we are making great commitments in service to others, this is never simply
because we only have the other in view. We remain
very much in the picture. We seek both acknowledgment and commendation. Sometimes, we seek our
own betterment and glory. These realities, however,
should not hinder us from repentance and service.
They simply remind us how much we need the grace
of God and how much we need to be transformed.
Transformation will be, therefore, an ongoing process.
But this is only for those who are prepared to face
themselves honestly in the searchlight of God's Word
and Spirit and in the light of life's experiences.

Reflection
*God is a master at taking the brokenness
of what we do and sanctifying it
with His presence.*

A Christian Ethic

*The Christian life is expressed in the rhythm of
freedom and responsibility. Without the former,
it lapses into legalism. Without the latter, it
becomes libertinism.*

There is an amazing movement in the Christian life.
Its beginning point is that we are saved from the
work of our hands. For no matter how much we strive
to achieve, we cannot find peace with God through our
good works, however good they are. Sooner or later we
must come to the realization that peace with God is apart
from works and that we are saved by grace through faith.

But that is not where the story ends. Ellul
believes that "all conduct in the Christian life can be
thought of only on the basis of the dialectical relation
between the two opposing factors of salvation by grace
and works."[5] Put more clearly, while we are saved by
grace, we live the Christian life in grateful service to
God and our neighbor.

Works, therefore, become inseparable from the
joy and responsibility of living the Christian life.
Service is never the extra in the Christian life. It does
not express a superlative commitment. It is the normal rhythm of the Christian life. It is the expression
of a thankfulness marked by obedience.

Action
*Do the will of God: This is the central
impulse to Christian ethics.*

A False Humility

*Spirituality is not self-rejection, but a denial of
self in order to do the will of God.*

We don't make God great by self-negation. This
is a false asceticism. This kind of piety operates
on the idea that the less we become, the more honored
God will be. This is a form of false humility. It manifests itself in many ways, including our praying. Ellul
speaks of the "prayer of resignation [where] I have no
genuine will. I am not a man who is standing upright,
struggling, working."[6] Such a prayer may appear to be
virtuous. But it is based on a false understanding of
who we are before God.

God never wills our nothingness, only our transformation. He desires not our self-negation, but our
cooperation. He does not want us to be helpless, but
empowered by the Spirit. He doesn't want prayers of
resignation, but prayers of passion. For we should neither resign ourselves before the awesomeness of God,
nor before the power of collective evil.

Before God, we should wrestle to know His will
and seek His blessing. In the face of evil, we should
stand in the strength that God provides.

Reflection
*Prayer always presses forward. It seeks what
we have not. It desires to be what we are not.
And it rejects what we may not.*

Political Involvement

Because Christ is Lord of all of life, Christian involvement in the arts, economics, and politics becomes a necessity.

Both as a citizen of a particular society and as a Christian, I am to be concerned with political issues. These lie within the sphere of Christian responsibility.

For many, the exercise of this responsibility is at a minimum in the casting of a carefully evaluated vote and in praying for the government. For others, there is the calling to a greater involvement—possibly the highest office in the land.

While individual Christians may feel free to work within particular political ideologies, the church as a whole can hardly identify itself with a particular political system. Instead, the church as a redeemed and prophetic community should constantly be encouraging and challenging the state in the pursuit of social and economic justice.

What should be avoided, however, is the dream to establish a Christian state. This is particularly the case because "no Christian political doctrine exists."[7] Nor, as Ellul insists, is there a Christian economic system.

But the Bible does speak to both politicians and economists. Not only is Scripture concerned with the appropriate use of power and the pursuit of justice, but also with a quality of life that enhances the family, cares for our neighbor, and responsibly uses the world's resources.

Action
Work to be free from power's intoxicating charm when working within the power systems of the world.

The Power of Method

*It is ever so easy to focus on methods, proce-
dures, and outcomes, but lose sight of the impact
on the people who are meant to produce these
outcomes and those who are supposed to benefit
from our programs.*

Ellul is adamant about one thing in particular:
"Technique has taken over all of man's activities."[8]
The modern world has been technologized and the
ramifications for people have been largely overlooked.
Productivity takes precedence over human consider-
ations and efficiency is celebrated as a law unto itself.

In the realm of the religious, technique has also
found a home. The church is no exception. Not only
are its very structures institutionalized, but much of
its life is technologized. Salvation is reduced to accepting certain spiritual "laws." Evangelism is wholly cast
in particular methods. Counseling has become dominated by techniques. And spirituality itself has been
reduced to various "stages."

Method should never lie at the heart of Christianity.
Relationship and reconciliation are, instead, its genius.
The love of God for each of us as individuals dissolves
the power of technique, but makes us wholly responsible to love God and our neighbor as ourselves.

Reflection
*Form and freedom must
complement each other.*

Judgment and Renewal

*If judgment strikes at the heart of what is
wrong, then the processes of renewal can begin.*

For many of us, judgment has negative connota-
tions. Judgment means criticism. It involves
censure. It can mean condemnation. Judgment, however, can be understood far more positively. It can mean
evaluation that leads to an assessment. This in turn can
lead to correction and eventually to renewal. While at
the end of time there is to be a final judgment, living
"in between" the times, we experience God's correction infused by grace.

In the words of Ellul: "God does not strike without healing."[9] Nor does He judge without mercy,
correct without love, rebuke without gentleness, and
discipline without having our development in focus.

None of this means, however, that we can pre-
sume on God's kindness. We may not sin lightly in
order to exploit God's grace and generosity. What it
does mean, however, is that at the point of our failure
there is always hope. For genuine repentance is the
beginning of change and confession always leads to
empowerment.

Reflection

*Christ's wounding and death led
to our redemption. At the cross,
judgment and mercy meet.*

Living Letters

However much we may wish to emphasize the importance of corporate action, the significant role of the individual should not be minimized.

We can fall into two errors. We can overplay the role of the individual and so return to the idea that heroes make history. On the other hand, we can so emphasize social and structural factors that we no longer have a place for purposeful human action. As Christians, we should maintain an emphasis on both. God works through both structures and individuals.

Some Christians, however, tend to be wary of what structures and institutions can achieve. Ellul is one such person. He believes that institutions easily assume a self-serving role and that they develop ideologies and mechanisms that make them self-perpetuating. He therefore writes: "It is not our instruments and our institutions which count, but ourselves, for it is ourselves who are God's instruments."[10]

Part of our responsibility, therefore, as servants of Christ is not only to work for the change of individuals through evangelism and practical care, but also to work for the transformation of the institutions in our society.

Reflection

Since the church is also an institution, we should continually work for its reformation in order that it may remain faithful to God, relevant to the wider community and be an instrument for social transformation.

The Good

*The good that we are to do is founded
on the goodness of God.*

There are different understandings of what is good. Some think that the good is to be determined by the majority in a society. Others claim that the good can only be what the individual wills. Others think that the good is what is beneficial for most people. And even where there are common understandings, there are different ideas as to how the good is to be achieved. While some think that the good can be achieved by any means, others rightly stress that the good can only be achieved by appropriate means. One can hardly, for example, build a just society by unjust means.

For the Christian, what is good must be determined by a wisdom beyond ourselves. As Ellul notes: "What is not acceptable to God is that we should decide on our own what is good and what is evil. Biblically, the good is in fact the will of God."[11] And the will of God is never simply a matter of outward precepts. It is never just a matter of not stealing. It also has to do with generosity. Sometimes, it may be a matter of selling all we have and giving it to the poor. The will of God has as much to do with our inner motivations as it is concerned with acts of service.

Action
*Achieve the good by joining mind, heart,
and hands to do the will of God.*

Urban Life

*Our desire to enjoy the benefits of the city while
turning a blind eye to its dysfunctionality shows
that we are living for present blessings rather
than for long-term gains.*

Ellul is highly negative about the city. Despite its archi-
tectural and cultural magnificence, the city is the
place where we celebrate our own achievements. We
tend not to see the city as the bonfire of vanities. Instead,
we celebrate the city as the expression of our technological prowess. Ellul believes that in this and other
ways, cities blind us to our need of God's goodness and
grace in our lives. Moreover, he finds a "parallel
between urban civilisation and warring civilisation."[12]

This is apt, particularly if we broaden the notion
of war by including the struggle for scarce resources.
And what a war this has become in our urban centers.
For some, this is a lack of educational opportunities.
For others, it is a lack of appropriate housing. For others in the mushrooming cities of the Third World, it
includes the struggle for adequate water. In this
struggle, the gap has only widened between the
"haves" and the "have-nots."

Action
*Pray for the welfare of our cities and
work for their redemption—but also
work for their humanization.*

Faithful to the End

*The walk of faith is not sustained by the swift
and the powerful, but by those who humbly
live by God's grace.*

It comes to all of us! With the process of aging comes
the weakening of our powers. And with retirement
comes the recognition that we are no longer as indispensable as we once thought. For some, the autumn
of life is filled with recrimination and bitterness. For
others, it is another stage in the journey of faith. And
those who traverse this part of the terrain most successfully are the women and men who have learned
to celebrate the grace of God.

Now is no longer the time for great exploits and
impressive achievements. Now is the time for grateful remembering and receiving small acts of kindness.
Now is the time to be led rather than to lead. Now is
the time to reflect rather than to do. And now is the
time to discover more fully that we are saved by grace
through faith and not on the basis of what we have
done. Ellul, in facing the reality of old age, writes: "I
must not give up, for the hour that approaches is the
hour of the truth of my life."[13]

Reflection
*If we have lived by the grace of God even
when we have done much, the autumn of our
life will only confirm how good God is.*

Free to Do God's Will

*The freedom that the Spirit gives is nothing
other than the empowerment to please God in
the midst of life.*

Freedom has little to do with doing what we want—unless, of course, some transformation has taken place in our willing and doing. For normally what we seek to achieve has little to do with God's concern for the world. We are usually more than preoccupied with our own concerns.

The work of the Spirit in our lives can change all of that. Our experience of God's love and grace cannot only deal with our sin problem, but can radically change us to embrace a whole new vision of life. And central to that vision is to live a life that is pleasing to God.

Ellul notes that in saving people, "Jesus sought to introduce them to the kingdom of freedom, i.e. to enable them to participate authentically in the will of his Father."[14] Doing the will of God has to do with obeying the commandments. But it goes deeper. Doing the will of God has to do not only with actions, but also with motives. And it has everything to do with the nudges of the Spirit that make doing the will of God concrete and specific.

Action
*Decide to do what we know must be done in
the light of Scripture, even though it appears
to be difficult. That is the will of God.*

Partnership

*While we participate in God's work, we are
never equal partners. We merely participate in
God's provision from beginning to end.*

Action in our world neither depends all on us nor
all on God. While there are times when God
chooses to work sovereignly and independently, He frequently chooses to work through people. But it is
whom He chooses: That is the surprise. Ellul rightly
notes that "God . . . is the One who elevates man to
the dignity in which he has a part in God's work."[15]

But God elevates those whom He wills. He does not
necessarily handpick our leaders and our heroes of faith.
He frequently chooses those we think are unlikely candidates. Yet these do have some common characteristics.
They are first of all women and men of humility. God
seldom uses the proud. He is not that impressed with
our achievements. Moreover, they are people of risk.
God can hardly use the careful. Those only concerned
with their own safety cannot do exploits for God. Also,
God uses men and women of hope who by faith can see
the contours of the new world.

Reflection
*God chooses those who are not
satisfied with the way things are.*

Faith and Belief

*While the God in whom one's faith is centered is
sure and steadfast, the journey of faith is characterized by risk and challenge.*

Ellul notes that "people who live in the world of
belief feel safe . . . [but] faith is forever placing us
on the razor's edge."[16] The reason for the contrast is that
belief is part of our religiosity. It is concerned with certainties. Faith, on the other hand, has to do with a
response to the revelatory power of Jesus Christ. This
faith commits us to the journey of obedience. It
involves accepting the Word of God against our own
common sense. It involves us in living a lifestyle
beyond the letter of the law.

Faith in Jesus Christ commits us to a person who
involves Himself in our lives through the power of the
Spirit. Faith is never simply intellectually accepting
certain doctrines. It has also to do with trust, commitment, and obedience. And this implies a journey
of risk and at times a walk of uncertainty. The only
thing that is certain about the reality of faith is that
Christ has gone before us and promises to sustain us
in the journey.

Reflection
*Faith is certain not because we so
faithfully exercise it, but because it is
God's gift to our fragile response.*

Self-Disclosure

We eventually make ourselves known in one
way or another. If our words do not disclose us,
our actions most certainly will.

There are private aspects to our lives that remain the province of those with whom we have an intimate relationship. But essentially, life is concerned with self-disclosure. This is intrinsic to who we are as creatures made in the image of God. For in life we are to reflect something of God's nature and we can only do this if we are open in our relationships.

Reflecting something of God's nature does not mean that we only show others the "good side" of ourselves. This is the mistake of those who only hold to triumphalistic forms of witness and service. We can also show our struggling self and so magnify the faithfulness of God. We can reveal our hurting self and so acknowledge our need of God the Healer. And we can also show our failing self and thereby claim that God alone is the One who forgives.

Ellul laments that in the modern world "the word is no longer a commitment and a disclosure of oneself."[17] Our use of language so often hides rather than reveals. And frequently we no longer call something by its proper name. Love frequently means lust, and justice is the exercise of might rather than right.

Reflection
Our words need to become
a vehicle of truth.

Acknowledging Limitation

While we are to celebrate and utilize the talents and gifts that God has given us, we are also to acknowledge personal limitation.

The idea that the Christian can be anything and do everything is clearly nonsense. While we need to become godly, we are not godlike. We will always remain creatures even in the life to come.

The divinization of the person is certainly not a Christian idea. One implication of our creatureliness is the experience of limitation. And this is nowhere better expressed than in the discipline of prayer.

Jacques Ellul writes that "prayer is specifically there for the purpose of setting a limit to our pretensions."[18] Prayer does remind us of our need and points us to God for His provision. It recognizes our powerlessness and seeks the Spirit's empowerment. It lays bare our lack of wisdom and looks to God for answers and direction. While prayer is never a negation of the self, it does acknowledge that we need God's involvement in every aspect of our lives. Although this does not exhaust the scope of prayer, true prayer helps us to focus on that which only God can do.

Reflection

In prayer we become more truly ourselves, for we don't have to pretend that we are more than that which we can do through God's help.

Is Being Good Enough?

Being good men and women won't necessarily change the world unless our goodness finds expression in the difficult cause of justice.

While some Christians continue to think that the way to godliness is withdrawal from the world, most rightly believe that they have some responsibility for their society. The dominant images that emerge from the New Testament are that God's people are called to be light, salt, and leaven. Thus, they are to have an illuminative, preservative, and transformative influence in the world.

It is one thing to acknowledge this at the level of ideas. It is another to develop meaningful strategies. One approach that is inadequate involves the idea that Christians will automatically better society if they live good lives. Ellul points out that "we must give up the idea that we can decrease sin by our virtues."[19] Goodness of itself won't change anything unless good women and men take action, become involved, challenge what is wrong, and promote what is right. Evil will still triumph when good men and women are silent and fail to take a stand.

Action
Our love and concern for others must challenge us to live lives of greater integrity, but must also move us to daring action.

Hearing a Different Drummer

Sadly, nonconformity is no longer regarded as a virtue. Living by the divine contrariness of Jesus has been eliminated from our religious vocabulary. Instead, we have become domesticated to obey religious leaders who cannot cope with healthy diversity.

Ellul states: "I have devoted my whole life to making people more aware, more free, more capable of judging for themselves, of getting out of the crowd."[20] Sadly, some contemporary Christians see this as a dubious cause to which to devote one's life. Yet it is a noble cause by any standard. The vision of the New Testament is to see people freed from sin and social expectations so that they can live boldly in the world.

A life pleasing to God is never a life of conformity except to take life in full stride and to walk the road of obedience to the Spirit's leading. A life with Christ as the new center point is a life that dares to say No to the powers of this age and the faulty values of our society. A life empowered by the Spirit dares to be different because there is not only a new vision of life, but strength to work toward its realization.

Reflection
Religious legalism was one of the powers that both Jesus and Paul sought to overcome.

False Hopes

Idolatry is alive in our modern technological world. One of its forms is celebrating our technological prowess, which is reshaping the very world in which we live.

While the "primitive" person stood in awe of the power of the elements and worshiped nature, "modern" persons worship the works of their own hands. In this sense, they are the greater idolaters and as such they are further removed from the life that has God as its center point. Jacques Ellul comments: "As long as there is a glimmer of confidence in these means [one's technological achievements], man prefers to stake his life on them rather than handing it over to God."[21]

In this sense, technology is a power that further alienates people from God. It is because we can now achieve so much that we think we need God less. However, the opposite is the case. The greater our power to change things, the greater is our need for wisdom from above. To put that differently, the greater our power, the more that needs to be directed within a framework of godly values.

Reflection
As we increase in the ability to affect and change our world, so our ethical responsibility increases.

Self-Identity

*In the light of God's redemptive love, I can discover
who I really am.*

Many in our modern world are overcome with self-doubt, uncertainty, and lack of identity. Their cry
is "Who am I?" in a world so full of change and in
which one experiences so much alienation and mean-inglessness. That our lack of identity has a spiritual
dimension follows from our being made in God's
image. Understanding ourselves has to do with seeing
ourselves in the light of God's creative activity.

But more is involved. Ellul writes: "This God sin-gularizes people, sets them apart, and confers on each an
identity comparable to none other."[22] It is in the light of
God the Redeemer and more specifically in the light of
God as my Redeemer that I discover my personal worth.

This God formed my very being and loves me. This
God has made me different from others and encourages
me to be myself in the light of His grace. This God chal-lenges me to express my life in service to others, while
at the same time empowering me with His Spirit.

Reflection
*Christianity does not preach self-negation,
but the placement of ourselves in the
service of the God, who both redeems
us and makes us more fully human.*

Looking for Answers

*Our attempts to find certainty in an uncertain
world cannot be gained by a reversion to magic,
but only by living responsibly in the light of
God's grace.*

Difficult times spawn prophets in the same way that
summer rains proliferate weeds. The greater the
human predicament, the more outrageous are the
claims of would-be messiahs. Jacques Ellul comments that when "the future is once again a hazardous
mystery to which there is no key [we fall back] on the
magician, on the political prophet, on the miracle-
working wise man."[23]

   None of this suggests that we should not listen to
those who are gifted with discernment. But it does suggest that we should not look for easy answers and quick
solutions. Moreover, we should personally live responsibly before God. We need to wrestle in faith with life's
difficulties. We need prayerfully to seek answers. We
need to face life and overcome our fears and excuses.

   This stress on individual responsibility does not
mean that we stand alone. But it does mean that we
stand in the midst of brothers and sisters as equals, not
as those needing to be rescued.

Reflection
*Answers to life's difficulties
are our responsibility.*

Too Late

*Neither our experience of God nor our experience
of church seems to have adequately prepared us
for creative engagement with the world.*

Not only has the comfortability of the church medi-
ated our experience of God: It has also blunted
our participation in the world. The church tends to
make God predictable and the world enjoyable. This
has much to do with the church's social location.

In the First World, the church is the product of
the suburbs where men and women live anesthetized
lives. God can therefore be seen as Comforter rather
than as Liberator, and the good things of the world can
be enjoyed while we avoid its problems and pain.

Consequently, our experience of God is mediocre
and our involvement in the world is for personal benefit and not social transformation. As a result, we are
not at the forefront of anything. Because we don't have
an adequate vision of God, we can hardly have a great
concern for the world.

As Ellul notes: "Very often it is only after others have
brought it into the open that Christians become aware
of a problem and then they climb on the bandwagon."[24]

Reflection
*Because God is deeply concerned about the
world, our worship of Him should always
lead us back into the issues of our time.*

New Possibilities

*Authentic freedom torpedoes the reliance on
group-think and mass opinion.*

Freedom has something to do with moving beyond
group opinion and accepted norms and practices.
Suspicion therefore serves the concept of freedom. It
calls into question the premise that those who are in
power have the only correct view of reality. Such "cor-
rectness" can only serve the interests of the status quo.
The first task of supporters of freedom, therefore, is
to create critical distance by calling into question the
way things are.

This does not necessarily lead to the wholesale
rejection of tradition, but it frequently leads to a
reshaping of those features of tradition that have
become oppressive. The creation of critical distance is
the mother of change.

Ellul correctly remarks that freedom is "the
coming of something new into the world."[25] And if the
new is to emerge, the old must be evaluated and the
power of its mystique broken.

Reflection
*The power of tradition can lull us into a
certainty that is never questioned.*

The Inner Life

*There is an intimate connection between our
inner and outer life. Holiness must express itself
in appropriate ministries and structures.*

Being and doing belong together. So do spirituality
and service. And appropriate structures must
express the inner values that we hold. Ellul asks:
"What is the good of maintaining the cultus and holy
things if the people itself is not holy?"[26]

Clearly, the answer to this question is complex,
for the maintenance of certain religious ceremonies—
even when our heart is not really in them—is
appropriate. In time, our heart may catch up. However,
there are also problems with maintaining outward
forms that don't reflect inner realities. In time, we may
unfortunately begin to live with the dichotomy.

A better way is to strive for a synchronicity where
the outer and inner realities harmonize. This means
that we can't call ourselves a community church if we
don't practice community and sharing. It means that
we cannot express exuberant praise when we are not
experiencing God's goodness, forgiveness, and grace.

Reflection
*What is in our hearts must come to
expression in our religious ceremonies.*

Justification

*One cannot use unjust means to build
a just society.*

The old agricultural principle that maintains a link between sowing and reaping is seldom applied directly to the moral world. In the world of morality, we more often use the principle "Do what you want as long as you don't get caught." In living this erroneous idea, we fail to see that we do always get caught. For in living out certain values, we shape ourselves into the very persons we are becoming. Even though we don't think so, the law of sowing and reaping is still at work. One could say that this law is a moral principle of the universe.

Yet the modern person is strangely resistant to this principle. He or she tends not to think of the consequences of certain behaviors as long as one is achieving and winning. Ellul points out that "in our day, everything that 'succeeds' . . . is justified."[27] But slowly this odd escapist idea is being undermined. We are beginning to realize that, if we continue to exploit the natural environment, it will turn on us; if we live immorally, disease will follow; and if we control but do not care, the social order will disintegrate.

Reflection
*When we exploit nature or the social order,
we may initially have much, but in the
end we stand empty-handed.*

The Wholly Other

*The way we typify God usually tells us more
about ourselves than about the Creator and
Sustainer of the universe.*

Throughout church history, various typifications of
God have predominated. In an age of kingly rule,
God was described as a king. In our time of insecurity and alienation, God is regarded as Father. And in
the light of the feminist movement, the fatherly
image of God has once again been modified to include
feminine characteristics.

This attempt to characterize God in terms of our
dominant social and cultural images is hardly likely
to go away. Succeeding generations will do the same,
but will evoke different metaphors. Depending on the
scientific development of the third millennium, God
may be thought of in much more cosmic terms.

None of this is inherently inappropriate. But there
are some problems. Ellul is concerned that "we think
about God with far too great familiarity."[28] I am concerned
that our view of God tends to be lopsided in that we stress
certain characteristics at the cost of others. Moreover, if
we typify God in the dominant images of our time, we
may well emasculate His transformative power.

Reflection
*We need to reemphasize the God who
encounters us rather than the God
of our rational apprehension.*

Humility

While we wish that we could say we have
succeeded, we have to admit that in many
ways we have failed.

The confession of failure need not be a negative
harping on human frailty. It need not be a somber
introversion. Instead, it can be a dignified admission
of human limitation. Jacques Ellul admits simply: "I
am human like everyone else, and I have failed some
of the tests of love and not met all the challenges."[29]

In this confession, there is nothing that authen-
ticates Nietzsche's criticism of Christians who make
a virtue of weakness. Ellul is making a simple statement of fact. We all fail. But we also succeed. We make
mistakes. But we also do what is right.

I do not want to make light of sinful behavior, but
much of what we do is not sinful; it is merely inadequate. Even when we are doing the will of God in the
power of the Spirit, we need to admit that we could
have done better. This neither elevates nor excuses
human wrongdoing. It simply acknowledges that we
don't always fulfill our highest intentions.

Reflection
Humility and realism
are intimately related.

Facing Reality

*The light of Christ does not turn us away from
the world. It empowers us to face life realistically.*

Under the blaze of Marxist criticism, Christianity
was typified as escapist, otherworldly, and irrelevant. Subsequent history has shown that Marxism itself
was unhistorical in that it completely failed to achieve
its ideals of transformation and human solidarity.

Marxism's failure, however, does not take the heat
off Christianity. In fact, the opposite is the case. For
the pressure is now on Christianity to get it right without the benefit of criticism from its staunchest
opponent. And the starting point of getting it right has
to do first of all with facing reality. For if we don't have
a realistic picture of ourselves and of our world, we can
hardly be the agents of social transformation.

Ellul is not so confident that we can become real-
ists. He writes: "A remarkable thing about even the active
Christian is that he never has much more than a vague
idea about reality."[30] He is right in that those of us who
are Christians are often naive and simplistic. Frequently,
we are simply idealistic. Sometimes we are escapist.

Clearly this needs to change. Instead, we need to
do our homework in achieving a penetrating analysis
as well as gaining a vision for change that reflects God's
kingdom values.

Action
*Embrace a vision of the new that harmonizes
with God's values as a basis for our social,
economic, and political action in the world.*

MAY

Who Am I?

*The courage to be is preceded by an answer to
the question: Who am I?*

Who am I? is a difficult existential question. It is
particularly difficult because, when I think I
have some answers, life's experiences call my certainty
into question. For who I am is not unrelated to my
experience of life. The question of my identity, therefore, cannot be settled in isolation. It is never simply
a theoretical question. It involves my very life.

Yet most of us would assert that we are more than
simply our experiences of life. We can point to those
who have experienced life's trials and misery and yet
are people of dignity and hope. This suggests a transcendent dimension.

Christians claim rightly that we are none other than
those who are made in God's image. Our life, therefore,
is sacred and unique. Our very existence presupposes
the creative and sustaining love of God. Yet many people
avoid pursuing the question of their existence.

Ellul notes one escape route: "My acts allow me to
escape the haunting question: Who am I?"[1] There are also
other ways of avoiding this issue. But because act and
being belong together, I finally cannot avoid the question
of my existence. And if what I do has meaning, then it
must be premised on the fact that I have meaning as well.

Reflection
*Who I am has a fuller meaning if
I am created for God's purposes.*

Integrity

In demonstrating our faith to the world, we are not saying how good we are. We are simply celebrating the love and grace of God in an obvious way.

Faith and life are interrelated. And faith in Christ must express itself in values and actions that point to God's kingdom. Ellul makes the observation: "A faith proclaimed in accordance with a faith lived increases faith tenfold."[2]

In this, Ellul is not only emphasizing that our faith needs to have practical expression, but more particularly that the doing of faith increases faith. Faith as an intellectual certainty needs to grow into a faith as trust. And faith that expresses itself in loving service is a faith that begins to structure itself in a particular rhythm of life.

This is not to suggest that faith is no longer decision, because the dimension of obedience never leaves faith. But faith can become a wisdom based on the many expressions of a life of obedience.

Action
Practice faith as a habit of the heart and a service of your hands so that it develops beyond faith as a mere intellectual reality.

Like Others

*Christians, like others, are caught up in the
same rhythm of life. They work. They marry.
They have children. They remain single. They
develop their careers and secure their future.
And they die.*

The life of the Christian, like most other people, is
quite unremarkable. We are begotten and we beget.
We create family and community and yet both have
preceded us and sustain us in our family and community-building. We work in order to sustain our life,
to express our giftedness and skills, and to make some
mark on the world. We encounter life's difficulties and
celebrate its blessings. We struggle with questions and
are grateful for some answers. As Ellul notes, for the
Christian, "the setting of his life is the same as that of
other men."[3]

Yet in other ways, the life of the Christian is remark-
ably different. It has God at its center. It is characterized
by faith. It is bathed in prayer. It is focused on doing God's
will. It is expressed in loving service. None of this means,
however, that the Christian easily sails through life. It
only means that, for the Christian, God is at the helm.

Reflection

*The only difference between Christians
and others is that, while many live in
revolt or disinterest, the Christian sees
God as central to life itself.*

The God of History

Spirituality embraces the real world as
the arena for action.

Ellul points out that "the Old Testament is utterly
'materialist'; God enters the concrete life of his
people and does not withdraw them from the world."[4]

The story of the Old Testament is the story of
God's participation in the real world. God enters the
suffering of His people in bondage and reveals Himself
as liberator. In the despairing wilderness journey, He
reveals Himself as the faithful provider. In cementing
the covenant, God is the compassionate initiator who
shows Himself strong on behalf of His people. And in
every aspect of Israel's life, God weaves a mosaic of
guidelines expecting Israel's obedient response.

But the genius of the Old Testament lies not in
what God tells Israel to do. It lies instead in God's participation in the common lot of His covenant people.
It is God's joining with His people that provides hope
for us. He also wishes to fully participate in our lives.

Reflection
God's involvement can only ever be
seen from the perspective of faith.

New Values

*Freedom in Christ subverts the old moralism
which, while it looks so right, fails to meet the
Law's intention to love.*

Outcasts are welcomed. Sinners are forgiven.
Extortionists repay what they have taken. Cultural
outsiders, like the good Samaritan, demonstrate neighborliness. The previously uninvited frequent the banquet
table. The inarticulate have their prayers answered. The
lost are sought out. The poor are blessed. And mere children are held up as examples of the kingdom.

Ellul notes that "in all the parables, the person
who serves as an example has not lived a moral life.
The one who is rejected is the one who has lived a
moral life."[5] Not only are kingdom values upside-down
values, but God has a habit of choosing the most
unlikely people. In doing this, God is neither foolish
nor presumptuous. He merely has a consistent policy
in confounding the wise of this world. He chooses the
powerless to show forth His strength and those whom
the world counts as nothing are raised up to show forth
His glory.

Reflection
*The good news of the Bible is that
the seemingly hopeless become
models of the grace of God.*

Peacemakers

*While peacemaking is a strategy, it is more
particularly a way of life.*

Peacemaking can be the broad strategy of nonviolent
resistance adopted by Gandhi and Martin Luther
King. It can also be a more small-scale strategy that seeks
to foster cooperation and harmony among individuals.
But peacemaking is always something more fundamental. It ought to be a whole way of life. Ellul notes:
"It is in being himself at peace that a man becomes
peaceful; it is in living the love of God that he becomes
capable of manifesting that love."[6] Peacemaking is thus
the expression of a life that is characterized by peace.

Because inner peace is never achieved by compromise but only by a life of integrity, the task of
peacemaking can only be marked by a passion for justice. Peacemaking is not achieved by a "peace at any
price" approach. Peacemaking, instead, sees its task as
building a better world. And in working toward this
goal, it sees an intimate connection between ends and
means. Building a just world requires just means.
Peacemaking involves peaceful means and that can
only come from those who are at peace.

Reflection
*When the Prince of Peace rules in
our hearts, He creates peace.*

Word and Miracle

In a world of difficulty we grasp for the miracle.
Instead, we should hear the word that points us
to the living Word, Jesus Christ. In Christ's
embrace, everything is a miracle.

People have always sought for the miraculous.
Even in our rationalistic, scientific, and technological age, this search has not abated. It may even have
intensified. For while we have overloaded the rational
mind, we have starved the human spirit. As a result,
the search for Utopian hopes, esoteric answers, and
miraculous cures continues.

The problem with the headlong rush toward the
miraculous lies in the fact that the miracle is meant to serve
us, not change us. The miracle is meant to fill the
gap, to meet our needs, and to provide the extra. But
it leaves us in control with our agendas intact. In other
words, we use the miraculous to serve our own ends.

Not so when we embrace the living Word. Christ
doesn't simply add another miracle to our lives. He
changes us. And this change is so fundamental that He
takes control and sets new priorities for our lives.

Ellul's comment is appropriate: "We have to
believe in God's word rather than the miracle."[7]

Reflection

There is no greater miracle than to be
embraced by the living Word.

In Whose Image?

*We long for savior figures, but then go on to
make them into our own image.*

We are strangely divided within ourselves. We want
the best, but so easily settle for the mediocre. We
strive for greatness, but so easily allow ourselves to be
compromised. We want to be honest, but so readily
bend the truth. We long for God, but so frequently prefer our own "idols."

And what of Jesus, the One we love and worship?
Well, Him we have domesticated. He is the heavenly
Christ who never agonized His doubts in the garden.
He is the gentle Christ who never drove anyone out
of the temple. He is the beautiful Christ who never died
a violent death. And He is the blessed Christ who never
called us to a costly discipleship.

Ellul identifies our problem as "making Jesus over
into the religious personage who suits us."[8] Somehow,
we can't leave Him alone. We will not allow Him to
confront us in His otherness. The very One who alone
can save us is the one we wish to control and remake.
And yet, if we will only allow Him to be who He is,
He will remake us in His gentle embrace.

Reflection
*The Christ of our own making will
soon cease to fascinate us.*

Guarding the Inner Life

There are some things that should be carefully nurtured in our inner life that are not the topic for public testimony.

Some things should remain hidden from others. These are not our wrongdoings. They need to be appropriately confessed to those we have hurt and wronged. What should remain hidden are our spiritual virtues. Our prayers, our generous giving, our painful commitments, our steps of obedience, and our experience of suffering should be maintained as the building blocks of our inner life.

They are not the material for public consumption. Ellul disparagingly comments: "In those spectacular conversions and spiritual sagas, the authors expose themselves directly, display themselves and blabber [about] what ought to be their most intimate secrets."[9]

This is not to say that there is no room for personal sharing and testimony so that others might benefit and be encouraged. The issue is different. Some things should remain hidden lest we begin to glory in our own generosity and obedience. Moreover, Christ should be our focus, not our own spirituality.

Reflection
The hiddenness of our inner life will always manifest itself anyway.

Secular Vocation

Spiritual ministry and secular vocation do not form a contrast for the Christian. One serves God either in the church or in the world. The one form of service is not higher than the other.

We love to make distinctions. Christians often claim that the priesthood or the church's ministry is a higher vocation than the teacher who seeks to serve God in the education system. Such distinctions pivot on an inadequate understanding of ministry. Ministry is not only that which serves the needs of those who frequent the church organization. Ministry involves any and every service that seeks to build the human community as well as the Christian community into a greater conformity with the values of God's kingdom.

Ellul emphasizes the role of the "layperson" who is "involved in the life of the world through his work and interests."[10] Such a person can be God's agent for change when work is done not merely for the purpose of economic survival, but to bring about God's good in the world. The Christian presence in all areas of life and in all the institutions of our land can have not only a preserving effect, but also a transformative impact.

Action
Prepare to serve God in any area of life. Whatever it is, it is a valid service when done to God's glory.

Self-Therapy?

While praying itself can bring a form of relief because we have articulated our concerns, this is not the real purpose of prayer.

Prayer is not talking to ourselves. It is not simply articulating what previously lay half-submerged in our inner self. Prayer is not, as Ellul points out, a form of talking where "self-therapy takes place."[11] This idea of prayer means that we are in charge and can simply help ourselves.

Prayer is, in fact, quite different. While it is valuable to express our fears or our needs, the focus of prayer is that we express these to God. In so doing, we are acknowledging God's grace and power, believing that He will respond to us in His wisdom and concern. This does not mean that God will always give us what we want. Prayer never compels God. It simply acknowledges our need and invites God's loving participation in our lives.

Action
Make prayer a regular habit of life. Never leave prayer until there is desperation.

Creating Distance

While we can never be wholly objective and dis-
passionate, it is important to create distance in
order to have room for reflection.

Much of what we do happens in the heat of the
moment. Many decisions are made on the run
and many commitments are made lightly. Afterward,
we lament the fact that we did not take time to be still,
to reflect, and to create some space in which we could
have come to a more careful and prayerful decision.

Ellul comments that "a dispassionate stance is
always indispensable."[12] This is not to say that decisions cannot be passionately made. In fact, all good
decisions need to be characterized by courage and conviction. But for a decision to be truly passionate, it
needs to be based on more than the heat of the
moment. It needs to be based on a careful reflection
that counts the cost and has some awareness of the
consequences. Thus true passion is fortified by a dispassionate reflection that gives passion its necessary
depth to walk the long road.

Action
Make careful decisions
rather than rash vows.

Contradictions

*Not even for the Christian does everything
become clear, smooth, and noncontradictory.*

Christians also live with tensions and paradoxes. In
fact, they may even experience these in an aggra-
vated way. For having experienced God's salvation,
they are yet to grow into its fullness. Having been freed
from sin's power, they are to put off wrongdoing. Living
in the circle of God's safety, they yet experience life's
trials. Knowing God's blessings, they also experience
pain and disappointment.

Jacques Ellul makes the general observation that
"reality includes positive and negative things. It includes
contradictory things that do not exclude one another,
but coexist."[13]

For the Christian, this also remains the case. The
most basic reason for this is that the Christian lives
between the times: between the disempowerment of
the old order and the "yet to be fully established" reality of God's final kingdom. The Christian thus lives in
the reality of God's irrupted order: the coming of God's
reign in a sinful and rebellious world.

To be in such a place is never without its tensions.
But it is also full of possibilities to see the new come
into being.

Reflection
*The paradoxes of life at least prevent
us from coming up with easy answers
that do not fit life's complexity.*

A Future Generation

*Stewardship is intimately bound up with a
responsible accounting that leaves the next
generation in credit.*

The continued escalation of the world's population,
the persistent greed on the part of the First World
to have more than a lion's share of the world's
resources, and the continued dwindling of those
resources has forcibly brought home the questions:
What kind of world are we producing? What kind of
world will our children inherit?

Sadly, for some, these questions are of no concern.
In the words of Ellul, these people "exist in the present
moment and have no will for anything else."[14] This cannot be a Christian stance, not even for those who believe
in the soon return of Jesus Christ and the end of the age.
For as stewards who are accountable for God's world, we
have a mandate to enhance the world, not to destroy it.
We are to be caretakers, not exploiters. We are to responsibly develop, not technologically distort our world.

Action
*Put energy into earth saving, not only
soul saving. For too long, the Protestant
work ethic has reinforced the idea that
subduing the earth meant exploiting it.*

Opposing the Powers

Rather than baptizing the existing powers,
Christians should actively work for their
transformation.

Christians are grappling with making their faith relevant for all of life. Christian perspectives on technology, economics, politics, and other aspects of social life are being explored and developed. These are good signs. Christians need to emerge from the safe cocoon of the ecclesiastical ghetto and become the scattered church in the world in their Monday to Saturday experience of life.

What needs to be avoided, however, is that Christians too quickly bless a particular economic or political perspective. Ellul asserts that "the biblical view is not just apolitical but anti-political, in the sense that it refuses to confer any value on political power."[15]

This appears to be an overstatement, because God uses government for the good order of society. However, God's commitment to government does not necessarily mean His blessing of a particular political system. And because most political systems have problems, Christians may serve such systems better by challenging the system to greater accountability and justice than by enjoying the fruit of political privilege.

Action
Work from the margins in the quest for political
change. This may be a safer position than
to work from the seat of power.

Living the Tension

To love the world as God loves it is the way to involvement without compromise.

Christian thinking and practice is subject to the pendulum swing. In the nineteenth century, the God of liberalism was the immanent one. In the twentieth century, Karl Barth sounded the trumpet call for seeing God as transcendent and Wholly Other. Similarly in ministry to the world, Christians have at times embraced a pietistic withdrawal. At other times, they have developed the social gospel.

The truth frequently lies somewhere in between. Ellul notes that "the attempt to assimilate world and faith to each other is one mistake, and the attempt to separate them radically is another."[16] This calls Christians to live the tension. They plunge themselves deeply into the needs and concerns of the world, because their lives have been deeply touched by the caring heart of God. Their love for the world springs out of their love for God and gives their ministry its direction. For Christians do not simply want to do good in the world; they want above all else to do God's good, which has everything to do with transformation, based on mercy and justice.

Action

Purposefully engage the world in the spirit of freedom that comes from not being part of the world and its values and priorities.

The Divided Middle

*Even though the mind with its rationality
speaks so persuasively, the heart whispers a
different wisdom.*

In an age when science has explained so much and
controls so much, people are not wholly satisfied with
the answers and look elsewhere for meaning and hope.
It is almost as if we doubt the best that we have produced. It is as if we intuit that our technological
achievements do not fully reflect the nature of our being.

And so we dream different dreams. Ellul points
out that "man, swept along by science, is certainly not
stripped of his illusions, his childish belief, dreams,
reveries, uncontrolled passions, and myth-making."[17]

Sadly, these dreams don't bring us much further.
For while they reflect the creative side of our being, they
also reflect our divided selves. For we don't integrate
our science and our reveries. And to the extent that we
don't, we only increase our tensions and dividedness.

Reflection
*Neither science, nor our own myth-making,
should determine our vision of life. But a
vision of the kingdom of God, where all of life
subject to God's lordship should shape our
reflection and action in the world.*

God's Otherness

*God both reveals and withholds. God's
withholding leaves Him in control.*

Jacques Ellul notes that "when you try to pin God
down, he declares 'I am who I am.'"[18] And this highlights precisely the point at which God withholds
Himself. He loves to reveal Himself to the seeker. He
draws close to the wounded with healing and restora-
tion. He seeks the wanderer. He empowers the poor.
But God resists our attempts at control and manipulation. He does not dance to the tune of our questions.

But even to those to whom He draws close, God
remains the mysterious One. We apprehend Him by
faith, reflect on His Word, and experience His involvement in our lives but, even so, we only catch a glimpse.

This does not mean God is unconcerned. His
withholding does not reflect a withdrawal. It merely
sets the boundaries for an appropriate relationship
where God's sovereignty and our humanity are
respected.

Reflection
*God's "I am who I am" confirms His
mystery, not His unavailability.*

Never Enough

When all has been done in the difficult task of gospel proclamation and social transformation, Christians can never rest on their laurels. For success brings with it its own set of problems.

There is a certain blessing in being in a minority position. You can afford to be bold and brave in your suggestions regarding change. Things are different when you come to power. You quickly discover that significant change does not come all that easily.

Ellul believes, however, that the Christian should always be in opposition even when he or she is able to exercise power. He writes: "Even when the institutions, the laws, the reforms . . . have been achieved . . . he still has to be in opposition, he still has to exact more."[19]

This is a pertinent observation. Not only can change for the good in time become subverted, but change is never complete, for it seldom benefits the poor and marginalized. Moreover, change in one part of the social system usually results in problems in other areas. Because the task is never complete, it means that we must set our eyes on an obedient faithfulness rather than on transitory success.

Action
Work as a change agent, but recognize that the work is never done.

The God Who Empowers

*We need God's enabling and blessing not only
for what we cannot do, but also for that which
we can do well.*

God is not the God of the gaps. We cannot desire
Him only at the point of our inability or need. God
is not simply the divine rescuer or the cosmic Mr. Fix-
it. God seeks to be central to the whole of our life. He
seeks to be part of our joys as much as our sorrows.
He is involved in our health as much as in our need
for healing. He has a part in our abilities as much as
in our need and weakness.

We need God's participation in every aspect of our
life, including our prayers. Ellul notes that "it is God
who gives our prayer its value and its character, not our
interior disposition, nor our fervour, nor our lucidity."[20]

This does not mean that we can pray however we
like because God will understand. Rather, it means that
our most fervent and faithful prayers need to be
redeemed by the grace of God. For, at best, they are
but a small and weak offering.

Reflection
*God is never offended by our weakness
and vulnerability. He is not impressed
by our pride and self-satisfaction.*

World and Church

Christians frequently think when it comes to bless-
ings that it is the church that provides them. But
sometimes the world is a blessing to the church.

There is no doubt that the church is called to be a blessing to the world. God wishes to use the church as an agent of reconciliation and transformation. But this does not mean that all virtue lies with the church and that the world is wholly bad. Such a neat polarization does not fit the observable facts. Sometimes, the church is quite reactionary and movements in the world for justice and peace are far ahead of the church in both ideology and practice.

Jacques Ellul notes: "The world itself once again seems to be God's instrument in forcing the church to face up to its conscience."[21] The church should not be afraid of the world's corrective and challenging role. While the world can add nothing to the church's message of salvation, the world, marked by God's common grace to all, can challenge the church at the point of its integrity and consistency.

Sometimes the church has lost some of its own truth. The world has a way of reminding the church what that truth ought to be. At Christians' own peril, they fail to listen.

Reflection
The church cannot learn from the worldliness
of the world. But it can learn from the world
where God's common grace is manifest.

The God of Compassion

God's desire to grant to women and men the kiss
of reconciliation seems to know no bounds.

Ellul notes that God "does not withdraw from even the worst of men."[22] This can be put much more positively because God, in fact, strenuously reaches out toward us. While we may actively throw ourselves into His embrace, He was already visiting us before we began the journey home.

The sad thing is that sometimes "bad" people make the journey back to the Father's heart more confidently than "good" people. This is not only because good people are so stuck-up that they don't recognize their need for God's compassion and grace. Sometimes good people feel so bad that they think there is no hope for them. Sometimes good people seem to be more lost than those who are bad.

We, therefore, need to expand the above quote. God also does not withdraw from the best of people who sometimes more urgently need God's benediction and grace.

Action
Come home, no matter how good or bad
you are. All of us are equally lost.

Promise and Fulfillment

*In this life, there is no endpoint to the spiritual
journey. Having made progress, we may have to
relearn the old and familiar paths. At other
times, we are called to journey onward.*

God is much more than the God of the past who
showed His faithfulness to our ancestors. He is
also the God of the present who journeys with us in
our joy and pain. But, equally importantly, He is the
God of the future who calls us into His future plans
and purposes. The movement of the Christian life,
therefore, involves an appreciation of the past, a
thankfulness for the present, and an anticipation of the
future. It is the latter dimension in particular that fills
us with hope.

Ellul notes that the Christian life moves "from
promise to fulfilment and that the fulfilment contains
new promise leading to fulfilment."[23]

Fulfillment is, therefore, not a terminal point. It
is the seedbed for the further journey. Christians consequently cannot rest on their laurels. They are called
forward in a walk of discipleship and obedience.

Action
*Work on particular projects and programs,
but bear in mind that their completion is
simply the beginning of something else.*

Someone Else's Problem

*We tend to be easy on ourselves when we are
experiencing difficulty, but judgmental of others
when things are not going well for them. This
order needs to be reversed.*

Because we all experience failure, disappointment,
and difficulty, we find ways of coping and we
develop rationalizations and explanations. In most
cases, we have learned to be gentle on ourselves. When
difficulty comes our way, we attribute this to the fallenness of our world and express the belief that God
will bring something good out of this situation.

When considering another's difficulty, however, we
are frequently not so generous. We make statements such
as "I could see this coming"; "I am not surprised that this
has happened to him or her"; or "I always thought that
something wasn't quite right in their situation."

This form of judgmentalism, as Ellul notes, is
often compounded by the fact that we "very easily
accept the evil that befalls others."[24] It is as if they
somehow deserved it. Thus, while we strenuously
work and pray to overcome our own difficulties, we
stand idly by when others are not so fortunate. Christ
calls us to reverse this order.

Action
*Let us answer the call to enter another's pain
and difficulty as if it were our own.*

Passion and Truth

Neither truth without conviction nor conviction without truth are good alternatives. Rather, we should live truth passionately.

Sometimes, in the midst of our involvement in social change, things can become quite hazy. Our zeal may be intact, but our sense of direction is not. Our convictions may be strong, but our goals have become confused. More seriously, we may begin to lose ourselves in our much doing.

To maintain the long journey of social transformation, we need to be renewed along the way. And, equally importantly, we need to be sustained not only by a clear vision of our hoped-for goals, but also by the conviction of truth.

Ellul makes the point that "getting oneself killed for lies and errors doesn't make them true."[25] Nor does zeal make up for a lack of clarity. And active involvement by itself does not achieve much if it is not guided by a vision of God's kingdom and if it is not based on a love for God's truth.

Action
In the desire to change the world for the better, don't wait for the perfect plan or, on the other hand, rush ahead without any sense of purpose or direction.

From Moralism to Freedom

*Nothing is so ethically significant as the
freedom the believer has in Christ.*

Christendom has always been preoccupied with
developing moral guidelines for the faithful in
order to assist them in living the Christian life. Much
of this has frequently degenerated into a new legalism
that has merely repackaged an old moralism. And
instead of freeing people to live the radical values of
God's upside-down kingdom, this moralism reduced
them to the tired practice of a conservative ethic.

The challenge to live a life of obedient discipleship to the call of Christ is much more vital in its
outcome than to live by general moral principles.
These two should not be fully contrasted; but the call
of Christ does confront us with a deeper set of values.
We are not just forbidden to perpetrate murder. We
need to deal with hatred in our hearts. While moral
principles guide us to do no murder, Christ's empowerment assists us to overcome hatred.

Ellul's point is noteworthy: "The proclamation of
grace, the declaration of pardon and the opening up
of life to freedom are the direct opposite of moralism."[26]

Reflection
*Christian freedom is not less demanding
than moralism, but is radically different
in its essential impulse.*

Costly Involvement

*While we tend to go forth into the world with
our words, we should instead demonstrate the
Word made flesh.*

Ellul is emphatic that Christians "must plunge into
social and political problems in order to have an
influence on the world, not in the hope of making it
a paradise, but simply in order to make it tolerable."[27]
For some, this statement seems to be a minimum
requirement. They believe that Christians can and
should achieve a whole lot more. They believe that the
power of the gospel can transform whole societies.

It is true that masses of people in certain societies
have come to faith in Christ. But this does not necessarily mean that political and social problems are
adequately solved as well. The Christian answer does
not produce Utopia.

Frequently, social and political problems persist
or take a different form. This does not mean that we
give up on insurmountable problems. It simply means
that we keep working for justice and peace in a world
that so readily perverts these values.

Reflection
*To change the world, we must first bring
change in our own lives and communities.*

The Context of Hope

Hope can be born in the seemingly most impossible of situations. But it does not arise in the context of fear and suspicion.

Hope does not need hopeful circumstances to raise a vision for a better future. Hope can be born in the most humble circumstances. It can spring up in the most unlikely places. And frequently, it is possessed by the most unlikely people. Hope frequently eludes the rich and powerful. It often makes its home with the poor and needy.

But hope is never the natural inheritance of the poor. They, too, can be characterized by a deep despair. Hope, instead, is the magnificent gift of a beneficent God who empowers people to look to a future marked by grace and renewal. The recipients of such a gift are those who can do nothing other than hope. Such are the powerless who cannot afford the luxury of despair.

For to despair is to have nothing. And as Ellul points out, "There is no hope where suspicion is king."[28] Hoping against hope, the powerless receive the gift of hope as a gift that catches each one off guard.

Reflection
*Hope makes a
future possible.*

Into Your Hands

*We need to learn to entrust ourselves to one
another. But this works best when we have first
entrusted ourselves to God.*

In the practice of building the human community and
in the formation of Christian community, we are to
build bridges of understanding and cooperation. But
in the task of building a common life with a common
vision and with common goals, we must not destroy
individuality and difference. We cannot lose ourselves
for the sake of the group.

In this sense, Ellul is right when he remarks: "To
deliver man into the hands of man is the worst thing
possible."[29]

True community is not formed when we hand
ourselves over to one another. This simply makes us
potential candidates for exploitation. Rather, community is formed when we all submit ourselves to God
and, as a consequence, seek to serve each other. This
service is meant to free others and to empower them.
It is not meant to produce dependence and obligation.

Reflection

*The constant giving of ourselves to God
does not take us away from our neighbor.
It frees us to serve our neighbor without
domination and paternalism.*

The Whole Person

Human beings are loved by God in all the dimensions of their lives. The social and economic spheres of life do not fall outside of God's concern.

Christians readily believe that God is concerned about them spiritually. They also believe that, at the end of the age, God will totally transform them and fully take care of them. They are less certain about what happens in the meantime. For while they may confess that God is concerned about the whole person, they frequently experience fragmentation, deprivation, and alienation. Not only do they experience this in the world; it is frequently their lot also in the church.

This calls for radical change in their life together. For if the church, according to Ellul, "must no longer preach to the inner man alone, but to the whole man,"[30] then it must first practice such holism at home.

This calls for mutual care and sharing. More particularly, it calls for economic conversion. This means that both my heart and my resources are to come under the lordship of Christ. It means that what I have does not only belong to me, but is to be responsibly shared with brothers and sisters in Christ and others in need.

Reflection

In God's scheme of things, I am a steward rather than a possessor.

Answering Prayer

*Prayer is not talking ourselves into doing
that which we should do.*

Not only is prayer not self-therapy where we talk
ourselves into feeling better: It is also not a form
of self-motivation. Nor is prayer a form of planning for
our own involvement in social action.

Jacques Ellul rejects the idea "that man must himself perform that which he petitions."[31] While God at
times may wish to involve us in some aspects of the
things we pray about, it is to God that we look for
answers. And we can do so with confidence and trust
because God is both all-knowing and all-powerful. He
sees the larger picture. God also knows the true intention of our prayers. And He is able both to intervene
with His power as well as to bring together the various circumstances that work for His intended change.

This makes prayer an exciting adventure. It is our
playing a small part in a much bigger plot, a part that
surprisingly is significant, because God is pleased to
be attentive to the cry of His people.

Reflection
*In prayer, we should first come with
open hands so that God can fill them
with the concerns of His heart.*

JUNE

So That They May See

Christian action is often our own action that has invoked God's blessing. A more fully Christian action is that which is modeled on the words and deeds of Jesus.

Many Christians see the words and deeds of Jesus as relevant for their salvation, but not their lifestyle. This is because they believe that Jesus' words and deeds are unlivable. Only Jesus the Savior could live like that. We cannot for, after all, we are not divine. This rationale, however, overlooks the fact that Jesus, the servant leader, laid aside His heavenly powers and lived and ministered in the power of the Spirit.

We are also called to live and minister in the power of the Spirit. In this way, we also can go the second mile, forgive our enemies, work for another's well-being, and possibly even lay down our lives for our friends. Ellul points out that "we must see to it that our works proceed so directly from the action of Jesus in us, that the world will see them in that light."[1] This is only possible if we are empowered by the Spirit and order our lives as imitators of Christ.

Action
Live the words of Jesus, but only in the power of the Spirit.

Those Who Seek

The self-satisfied rarely receive the good things God wishes to give. The seekers, however, are candidates for God's surprises.

Jacques Ellul makes the general observation that "where man is not looking for anything, he cannot hear the gospel."[2] There are, of course, exceptions. Sometimes, God comes to those who do not seek. He answers those who have not yet formulated their questions. And He blesses those who have not yet recognized their need. But usually God's goodness comes to those who have had the spell of their own self-sufficiency broken. And He draws near to those who have come some way toward acknowledging their own need.

However, these steps are always partial and incomplete. When we are broken or guilty, we often do not know what we want or what we need. Our self-prognosis is often incomplete and we flounder in seeking to know what is best for us. But this is not a hindrance in our quest for wholeness. God meets us at the point of our desire and even at the point of our confusion. And He will carry us forward.

Action

Cry to God for help, even if it cannot be a fully knowing cry. The point is to call out nonetheless.

Domination

*In fulfilling the creation mandate to fill the earth
and to subdue it, we need to find responsible
ways in which to care for the world, which
sustains us.*

Ellul is adamant that the Western mind-set is
bewitched with the will to dominate. He writes: "No
human group has ever implemented so fully the will to
rationalise everything and to dominate the world of ideas
no less than the world of things."[3] This compulsion has
been a mixed blessing. It has been the driving force of
progress. It has fueled every form of exploitation.

Some would argue that the world cannot go on
without this impulse. No economic or political system
would survive without domination. And many
churches have adopted a similar mode of operation.

Jesus, however, points us in another direction.
Because He was the suffering servant and the servant
prince, He qualifies domination. Domination must be
linked to God's intention and, because God desires
mercy and justice, domination can never mean
exploitation. In fact, it can only mean a servanthood
that uplifts the needy from the ash heap of oppression.

Action
*Be a servant leader, viewing the long-term
benefit to others rather than the
immediate gain to yourself.*

Lord, Forgive Me!

*Extending and receiving forgiveness is one of the
most significant elements in our quest for
wholeness. More importantly, forgiveness should
be sought for its own sake, not for its benefits.*

Ellul is depressingly right that we all do evil: "We do
it to neighbours, spouses, prisoners, enemies and the
natural environment."[4] Even when we think that we are
doing so well, we still fail. In fact, we can safely assert that,
when the need for seeking and extending forgiveness has
faded from our lives, we can assume that something has
gone terribly wrong. And the worst scenarios are that we
have become blind to our own wrongdoing and that we
have become callused to the point where we don't seek
forgiveness for our own wrongs.

Locked into a pattern of not extending forgiveness
to others, we become bitter. Locked into a pattern of
not seeking forgiveness for ourselves, we become
guilt-ridden or indifferent. Either way, we slowly
destroy our inner life and our outer relationships.

Forgiveness, therefore, is not the occasional luxury that we extend to others or receive for ourselves.
It is the bread and butter of our very existence. It is
one of life's sweetest realities. It is God's greatest gift.

Action

*Seek forgiveness for wronging others and,
when appropriate, also the forgiveness
of the one we have wronged. Forgive
others when wronged by others.*

Discerning the Times

The yearning for holiness is not at odds with the desire for relevance. For while holiness sets us apart unto God, it is God who calls us into the world.

The desire for relevance should be the quest of every Christian, for not only do Christians partake in the affairs of the world, but their very life is sustained by the world. The world is their home as much as heaven is their destination. Therefore, Christians should desire to bring to the world something of the love that Christ has worked in their hearts by the Holy Spirit.

To do this effectively, Christians "must discern the genuine issues of our time"[5] and must involve themselves with the genuine concerns of people. We cannot have the one without the other. If we are only concerned with issues, we may remain at the theoretical level and do little to meet real needs. If we are only involved with people's needs, we may become overwhelmed with much doing and lose perspective and direction.

Love, therefore, cannot afford to be blind. It needs to be both discerning and practically engaging.

Action
Exercise discernment: This can lead to more relevant action.

Manipulation

*Christ has placed men and women in a free
place where they can respond in thankfulness
and obedience. We often place people in a situation of coercion to facilitate belief.*

In our eagerness to help people come to faith, we
often apply all sorts of subtle pressures. And in our
experience of church, we are sometimes, perhaps often,
subject to manipulation.

This occurs when some theological hobbyhorse
is being promoted or some program has been adopted
that requires the generous giving of the faithful. In
some instances, things do not stop there. The church
hierarchy seeks to control the whole of a person's life.
When this occurs, people are propagandized.

Ellul notes that "propaganda tries to surround
man by all possible routes in the realm of feelings as
well as ideas, by playing on his will or his needs,
through his conscious and his unconscious, assailing
him in both his private and public life."[6]

Our evangelism and our being church, however,
should be patterned more on the approach that Jesus
took. He did not call for commitment first and then
blessed people. He freely gave of His wisdom and healing, allowing people room to make their response.

Reflection
*A commitment based on freedom
will be a lasting commitment.*

With the Eyes of Love

*Love knows what careful analysis may
never reveal.*

Love can spring from a number of sources. It can
come purely from ourselves. It may be God's special gift to us. It can also be evoked by the other person.
Love is all the stronger when these various sources
merge. Love, however, does not simply provide us with
a new way of giving. It shapes a new way of being. It
affects us as much as those to whom we want to be loving. Love is, therefore, empowering and energizing for
both the giver and the recipient.

But love is also discerning. Ellul remarks that "it
is love alone that sees truly."[7] When we ask what love
can see, we find a number of answers. First, love sees
the other as worthy of love and this has all sorts of
immediate consequences, for we will give such a person honor, respect, and care. Second, love sees the
other's potential. As a consequence, we will give the
other encouragement. And third, love sees the other's
faults and therefore forgives and provides gentle but
firm challenge.

Reflection
*Love is one of the clearest windows
into our view of the world.*

The Gentle Yoke

*At one level, the commands of God seem difficult
and burdensome. At another level, they are
pointers to the only way of life worth living.*

While nonChristians looking in on the Christian
community can see the practice of celebration
and can discern a spirit of joy, their overall impression
of Christianity is best summarized by the word *austerity*. God is seen as demanding and the experience
of the Christian life is seen as a battle to be good and
virtuous when in fact we want to have a bit of fun.

Yet nothing is further from the truth. Ellul points
out that "what controls the world is not the oppressive will of a dictator God . . . but the total freedom
of the one who says 'my yoke is easy and my burden
is light.'"[8] The will of God should not be seen as that
which frustrates the expression of the good life, but
as that which directs it.

This does not mean that we will readily agree with
God's will. We usually experience the struggle of obedience. But when we move beyond our own selfishness
and stubbornness to embrace God's Word and direction,
we will find that it is the only wholesome way to live.

Reflection
*God's will is consistent with
the way we are made.*

The Risks of Faith

If there is anything that should characterize
Christians, it is that they be daring.
Unfortunately, Christians have learned to
be careful.

Christians can afford to be daring because in one sense
they have nothing left to lose. In joining with Christ,
they have lost everything. Their previous life, with its
values and priorities, has gone. In Christ, a new way of
being human and serving the world has come into view.

In another sense, Christians can be daring because
they have already gained everything there is to gain.
They have received new life through Christ and this life
will last into the age to come. All else will perish.

This realization should free them to take the risks
of faith while they live "between the times." Ellul makes
this comment: "What matters is whether Christians will
dare to risk everything in order to fulfil their function
in the world."[9] To this we can respond: The Christian
alone can afford to take risks because the old is no
longer relevant and the new beckons.

The fact that Christians are so often timid and conservative has nothing to do with their life in Christ, but
only with the way they are socialized into the values
of the family, church, or society.

Action
Live boldly! You only
get one opportunity.

Disciplining the Nations?

*While religious rulership finds expression in the
Old Testament theocracy and in the Middle Ages
church-state relationship, its ideology has been
subverted by the suffering servant.*

Discipling the nations sees evangelism as its tool
and the spread of Christian values as its goal.
Disciplining the nations is something quite different.
This position holds that Christians are best suited to
be in social and political leadership.

This view, though, is at best naive. At worst, it is
dangerous. Ellul points out that stewardship for some
"leads to a conception of leadership by divine right and
a kind of paternalism."[10] Christians in leadership can also
be mesmerized by the attractive sway of power. To make
matters worse, they may lack all kinds of political skills.

While Christians should be involved in all
spheres of life in order to manifest something of God's
kingdom, they would do better to take on a prophetic
or servant role. To challenge the system prophetically
or to serve the system subversively are better options
than to take the traditional path of power.

Reflection

*Disciplining the nations is a nostalgic longing
for a return to the days of theocracy. Those
days are long gone. We are called, instead, to
serve God faithfully in our pluralistic societies.*

Divine Jealousy

While jealousy commonly implies an unhealthy possessiveness that fears rivals, this is not so with God. His jealousy has our well-being in view.

Ellul rightly points out that God "cannot bear it that man should turn to someone other than himself."[11] This statement has all the elements of what one could expect to hear from your average jealous lover who clings tenaciously to a relationship in the face of threats from potential rivals.

But God's jealousy has a deeply caring dimension. It is like the nurturing character of mother love. But, more precisely, it is like parental love, which seeks to guide the teenage child after having relinquished the right to control the teenager's decisions. Its concern is that the teenager may make harmful choices.

Similarly, divine jealousy fears our straying after pseudo gods and the headlong pursuit of our own fancies, which finally leave us confused, unsatisfied, and disempowered. Yet even though so much is at stake, God's jealous love will only challenge and guide us. It will not control.

Reflection
*Divine jealousy sets the
parameters for caring love.*

The Open Ear

*Because faith has to do with the revelation of
God in the face of Jesus Christ, it involves
listening and receiving.*

I was brought up in a Christian family, but I had no
personal faith. In the midst of hearing the good news
of God's salvation, I somehow had not heard. I was like
a person suffering from thirst in a lake of fresh water.

How could that be, you may ask? The answer is
that my "inner ear" was not listening and the "eye of
faith" was not seeing. I was like a blind man with my
eyes wide open.

Faith is God's gift. It is a revelatory moment, never
simply an intellectual assent to certain scriptural
truths. Ellul is right, therefore, when he emphasizes
that "faith is . . . in the first instance, hearing."[12] It is
hearing something for the first time that I already knew,
but hearing it in a very different way. I hear it as the
truth for me. It is the truth that I must now embrace.
It is the truth that involves my very life.

Reflection
*Faith does not simply say Yes. It
takes on board this new insight
as God's answer for my life.*

The Christian Religion

*Christianity is a religion par excellence with all
the attendant trappings. But its real power does
not lie there. It lies in following the Christ of the
Galilean road.*

Christianity has been most skillful in developing its
religious infrastructure and superstructure.
Buildings, liturgies, priestly caste, dogmas, and values
are all carefully in place, providing the follower with
a sense of awe and structure.

Ellul rightly notes that "Christianity is being sub-
merged under the enormous religious wave of our
time."[13] To this we should add that Christianity has frequently added its share to the world's religiosity.

Yet strangely, Christianity's founder was characterized by a strong antireligious bent. He replaced
buildings with community, liturgies with purity of
heart, priestly caste with sisterhood and brotherhood, dogmas with faith, and values with obedience.

Jesus came to disturb the religious system, not to
enhance it. He did not create a religious alternative to
the old and tired Judaism of His time. He proclaimed
a whole new way of life.

Reflection
*We are better at developing religious
systems than in following the Christ
who calls us to obedience.*

Think Globally, Act Locally

Jesus had a vision for nothing less than the kingdom of God. Yet He responded to specific needs and situations.

It is true that global issues impact on local affairs. And we need to be aware of the large issues as we fight oppression and discrimination. Yet the sphere of our practical involvement has to be at the local level. Ellul observes that "by thinking globally I can analyse all phenomena but, when it comes to acting, it can only be local and on a grassroots level if it is to be honest, realistic and authentic."[14]

In the final analysis, significant action must have a human face. It is a response to particular people with particular struggles and issues who are part of a particular community. In fact, it is our immersion in the local community and its strengths and needs that helps us to think more carefully about the bigger issues. In standing with the community, we can see more clearly how particular policies have impacted on the life of such a community. It is from this perspective of local involvement that we can fight global injustice.

Action
Act locally and your global thinking will become relevant.

Good News for the Poor

*The realization that my present condition need
not be my final condition is the beginning of
liberation.*

A change of circumstances can go some way toward
bringing about change. But it is seldom deep and
lasting.

A more radical form of change is a change of consciousness. This involves looking at the same social
reality, but with new eyes. It sees the old in the light
of what it could be or should be. Ellul notes that "once
Christianity had destroyed the idea of destiny or fate,
the poor realised that . . . their condition was not
inevitable."[15]

Nothing militates against change more than the
idea that certain social arrangements are scripted by
destiny. And nothing invites change more than the idea
that God is the great change agent who invites us to
join Him in establishing the values of His kingdom.
And nothing makes that more concrete than the idea
that God is on the side of the poor, seeking their well-
being and deliverance.

Reflection
*A change of consciousness can occur when the
smooth flow of tradition is interrupted by
issues pressing for new answers.*

Inadequate Solutions

Christian solutions to solving the world's problems
are no better than that of others. They are only
better if God takes them up and blesses them.

There are Christians who believe that they have the answers for the world. For some, the answers lie in prayer on behalf of the world. For others, it is large-scale revival. For others again, it is the practice of social justice. And for some Christians, hope lies in the adoption of particular political and economic systems.

But answers to the world's problems do not lie in one or all of these strategies. Ellul comments that "we perceive the inadequacy of human solutions."[16] This includes all Christian solutions, for we cannot rectify the world. This is not a call to resignation and inactivity. It is a call to resist Utopianism.

Instead, the Christian approach to the world should be characterized by a blunt realism. Some, by God's grace, will be saved. Sometimes, the light of revival will temporarily flicker brightly. The fight for social justice will sometimes prevail and political strategies may for a time be better than others.

But the struggle will always continue until the end of the age.

Action
Take up the call to work for the world's
renewal in faith and hope, even though
we cannot finally change it.

The Silence of God

*In both our personal journey of faith and that of
the church, Christians experience the silence of
God as much as His revelation.*

While having the Word of God in our hands, we
can still be met by God's thunderous silence.
This is because the Word does not guarantee presence,
in the same way as a couple talking does not guarantee true fellowship. The impact of the Word depends
upon relationship. Sometimes, it is we who disturb the
relationship and render the Word mute and ineffective.
But sometimes God meets us in silence.

Ellul puts it much more strongly. He claims that
there are times "that God has turned away from us and
is leaving us to our fate."[17] This may happen when we
have persistently resisted the grace of God. But even
when no such disobedience has come into play, God
may well withdraw and lapse into silence.

Such a silence is never petulant or capricious. God
is certainly not playing a cat and mouse game. Nor is
His silence necessarily a form of punishment. It may
simply be His way of dealing with us so that we will
once again hear His Word with vigor and clarity.

Reflection
*Silence may well be the
gateway to new hearing.*

Holistic Ministry

*As our wrongdoing has created great social and
ecological disasters, our strategies for restora-
tion need to be comprehensive.*

Both our individual and our corporate sinning has
run as a fault line through our social fabric. Its negative ramifications are everywhere manifest. Not only
is personal morality infected, but our social and
political structures bear the marks of oppression, alienation, and injustice. Even the earth bears the scars of
willful exploitation. Ellul comments: "This earth,
having been ravaged, is no longer just a garden. It is
also a place of tragedies and disasters. Our task is to
restore it to itself."[18]

This calls for a holistic approach to ministry. As a
consequence, "soul saving" must have an outworking
in simple lifestyle and downward mobility. Being a
Christian involves participation in the formation of communities of justice. And such communities must model
the celebrative and caring aspects of stewardship by taking a stand against all forms of wanton exploitation.

Action
*Begin to practice responsible stewardship at
home and church. From the basis of our
practice, we can begin to challenge
the policy makers of our land.*

No Compromise

*The downhill slide usually occurs because
many small compromises have been made
along the way.*

A life of integrity comes with a price. A life lacking in
integrity exacts an even heavier price. Either way
we pay. The former style of life places truth above convenience. It does not place self-interest above meaningful
causes. The latter style of life fumbles with the truth. It
grasps its suspect goals no matter what the cost.

In the heat of the moment and in the pressure of
the situation, one's integrity can easily be undermined
and compromise becomes the ready option.

Major commitments and decisions should, therefore, not be made at such crucial moments. They need
to be forged in the place of solitude and prayer. Ellul
rightly notes that "the only respectable human decision is to refuse all compromise in advance."[19] For that
to occur, the formation of a clear vision of life's essential values must be in place beforehand. And these
must be kept in the face of great odds.

Reflection
*While application and fine-tuning should
occur in the warp and woof of life, one's
essential values remain the beacon light.*

The Test of Faith

*The journey of faith calls us to do the impossible,
which only becomes a possibility because of the
power of God's promises.*

Faith is not just a feeling. Nor is faith a simple trust
in the words and promises of some authority figure. Faith has a "revelatory" dimension. The emergence
of faith has to do with the impact of Jesus Christ, the
living Word, on our lives.

This impact is not peripheral. It strikes at the very
core of our existence. Ellul notes that "faith . . . puts
to the test every element of my life and society; it spares
nothing."[20] Faith does not add something extra to our
lives while leaving everything else intact. Faith revo-
lutionizes us.

We can never be the same after our encounter
with Jesus Christ, the living Word. It is not simply a
matter of adding a new spirituality or a new belief system to our lives: There needs to be a whole new way
of living our lives.

The result of our encounter with Christ and His
ongoing work through the Holy Spirit means the emergence of new values and priorities that radicalize
everything. Not only do we become different, but we
gain a new vision of what this world should be like.

Reflection

*Faith is not a passive quality. It means faith in
Christ and this involves actively following Him.*

Freeing the Word

Scripture contains a subversive theme: God's kingdom calls into question all our institutional values, including those of the church.

Whether we look at the Old or New Testament, the message is patently clear: Prophet and priest are pitted against each other. The latter serves the religious system and insists on the status quo. The former serves the renewing Word of God and calls for change and renewal.

The implication is that often the Word and the institution are at loggerheads. Ellul comments that "the word spoken by God in Christ is undoubtedly modified by the church."[21] Here, the institution seeks to control the Word and make it the servant of the system.

The opposite, in fact, should be the case. The institution should be subject to the Word of God and should define its vision and structures accordingly. At issue here is that the Word must be free to do its transforming work. This entails that the Word must not remain the province of the religious specialists. It must become the book of the people who believe that God has not only acted decisively in the past, but continues to act in the present.

Reflection
The Bible is more concerned about those who are oppressed by religious institutions than that it seeks to promote such institutions.

The Good

While there are vestiges of the good in our common life, God's quality of good is radically different.

The familiar objection that the church has often failed to do good in society and therefore Christianity has little to offer is clearly nonsense. This is a case of throwing out the baby with the bath water. Christianity has much to offer. And its vision of the good is not only life-changing, but also socially transformative.

The problem is that the church so often fails to believe and live its own message. This is because the good news in Christ is so different. Ellul writes: "What need would there be for a revelation if the good were registered in nature?"[22]

God's good is no ordinary good. It requires a revelation. It calls us to forgive rather than to retaliate. It calls us to serve instead of furthering our own goals. It calls us to community rather than to individualism. It calls us to holiness rather than compromise. It calls us to participate in the kingdom of God rather than to build our own systems and institutions. And it calls us to work for change in the world so that it will reflect God's values of justice and mercy.

Reflection
God's good can only be done by those made good by God's grace.

Rejected

*The figure of Jesus is deeply embedded in our
consciousness and culture. We can hardly shake
ourselves loose from its demand and are thus left
with one of two options: embrace or reject.*

Ellul, writing from a Western perspective, asserts:
"It is in our day that Jesus is, in the fullest and most
radical sense, being rejected . . . in every area of man's
endeavours: his thinking, his willing, his undertakings,
his building of his world."[23] In the West, Jesus the won-
derworker pales in the light of our technological
successes.

Jesus appears to be no match for our progress. . . .
Or is He? Maybe He can meet a need that is more fundamental. Maybe He can form our character and shape
our values in such a way that our successes no longer
exploit and dehumanize. Maybe He can inspire us to
work for a more just world and not simply be preoccupied with our own self-interest. Maybe He can
empower us to overcome personal and structural evil
and so work for a common good that saves us from
the destructive work of our own hands.

Reflection
*Our "maybes" can only be answered in
the embrace of God's grace in Christ.*

On Which Side?

*In the final analysis, we cannot please
everyone. We have to take sides.*

We have somehow caught the erroneous idea that,
because we are to love everyone, we are to adopt
a nonpartisan stance. Consequently, we have made a
virtue of neutrality. We have assumed that, as
Christians, we are to be on everyone's side and against
no one. As a result, we have had an anemic influence
in the world as far as social justice is concerned.

Clearly, we cannot play life's game both ways. We
have to make choices. And we will either serve the status quo or be those who work for constructive change.
We will either serve the poor or support the pharaohs
of this world.

Ellul is clear in his commitment. "My decision,"
he writes, "is to side with the poor."[24]

This decision came not only from his own childhood experience of poverty, but also from his reading
of Marx's critical sociology, which identified the poor
as alienated from the modern conditions of life. But,
more particularly, it came from his reading of Scripture.
God is the God of justice and therefore hears and
answers the cry of the poor.

Action
*Side with the poor, not simply to give
sympathy or aid, but to empower
through participation.*

Prayer in the Spirit

Prayer is much more than addressing pious language to God. It is a cry of the heart.

Prayer remains difficult for the person from the First World. Our progress and achievements have blinded us. We foolishly think that for so many aspects of our life we no longer need God. Prayer is not so difficult for the person in the Third World. Life's vulnerability drives them to prayer.

But prayer is so much more than simply addressing our needs to God. It is a language of the heart. It is the cry for intimacy. It is the yearning for companionship. It is spirit communing with spirit. Prayer essentially is a spiritual activity.

Ellul points out that "it is the entire prayer which is the prayer of the Holy Spirit."[25] Prayer is an activity in the Spirit and, as such, it frequently goes beyond words. It is a joining of our inner self with the yearnings of the Holy Spirit. Thus prayer is a giving of ourselves to the work of the Spirit. And this being carried by the Spirit may issue in fervent articulations, quiet reflections, ecstatic worship, and clear revelations.

There are no boundaries to the act of prayer when we catch the wind of the Spirit.

Reflection
In prayer, we move beyond
ourselves to the heart of God.

God's Action

It is inadequate to say that in the past God's action in the world was overt and now it is hidden. God has always been the One who both reveals and hides.

In our day as well as in the days of the Bible, God has worked overtly in the world. This can be seen not only in people coming to faith in Christ and in the signs of personal healing and deliverance. It can also be seen in historical movements that trumpet the cause of justice and condemn the blinding ideologies that promised people so much, but gave them stones for bread.

However, the signs of God's overt action do not exhaust God's involvement in our world. He also upholds all things. This aspect of God's work is without human instrumentality, although we are called to be partners with God in caring for the world. But in many other ways, God solicits our involvement. Ellul makes the following comment: "God rarely acts in a direct and transcendent manner; on the contrary, as a rule he chooses a human instrument to accomplish his word."[26] And even more frequently, God uses many different people in many different ways to express His compassion and concern for the world.

Action
*Do the world good by
doing God's bidding.*

The Image of God

God, the hidden one, is the One who reveals
Himself in all that He has made, especially in
those who are made in His image.

Man alone is not made in God's image. This would mean that the woman is the image of man. Both the woman and the man reflect the image of God. Both have a part to play in shaping and ruling God's earth. Both are to play an equal part in building Christian community.

Ellul notes that "the basic responsibility of both men and women is that the image of God should be present on earth."[27] This means that something of God's glory is reflected in the responsible stewardship of both the man and the woman in fulfilling their respective callings and exercising their gifts. Neither the man nor the woman alone can fully reflect the image of God. In a partnership in Christ, they do reflect God's image.

While we can never completely express God's image due to our own imperfections and the brokenness of our world, we can facilitate its expression. We do so when we emphasize participation, cooperation, and loving service as we proclaim and express practically the life we have in Christ.

Action
Replace domination by partnership
so that God's love and care can
be revealed in our world.

The Lordship of Christ

*Christ is to be Lord of our individual lives as
well as of the institutions and structures of
our society.*

Saved by the grace of God in Christ Jesus, Christians
can only relate to Jesus as Lord. Christ now has the
authority to direct their lives. And they have the opportunity to respond to His callings in faith and obedience.
Christ's lordship practically expresses itself in a life that
seeks to do His will.

Christ's servant rulership, however, is not only to
be exercised in the life of the individual Christian or
that of the Christian community. It must also find
expression in the wider community. Ellul remarks: "I
believe that Christ the Lord has to be proclaimed anew
in the face of all the lords of this world."[28]

These lords take many forms. They can be powerful ideologies, political systems, scientism, and our
technological prowess. They can also be religious systems that no longer magnify the grace of God in Christ.
In the face of all modern idolatries, we need to call
people to move away from their alluring power to
accept the gentle yoke of Christ.

Reflection
*The rulership of Christ liberates.
It does not oppress.*

Common Sense

The Christian is not only a creature of faith,
but also a person who needs to respond to
the real world.

Many of the conceptual polarizations that we have made are simply inadequate. It is true to say that Christians are to focus on a heavenly reality. But they are also called to demonstrate a practical concern for the world. Christians are to be women and men of prayer. They are also to be people of action. Christians are to live in faith and hope. They are also to be involved in the real issues of our time. More basically, Christians relate to God as both Redeemer and Creator.

They are, therefore, part of the Christian community as well as the human community. Being members of both communities frequently involves the Christian in tensions. The desire of the Christian, however, is to live a life of faith in both communities. But, as Ellul points out, this does not exclude the fact that "commonsense is useful."[29] Faith always has homespun practicalities. And our common activities are not outside of the realm of faith.

Reflection
Faith brought Lazarus
back to life. Common sense
unwrapped the graveclothes.

Domination

Domination takes many forms. The most subtle is ideological domination.

Corporate or collective sin in our world has very much to do with domination. Christ's agenda is totally the opposite. He calls for participation and equality. The Western world has well understood domination. In spite of its centuries of Christianization, it has hardly begun to understand the Christian alternative. This is because, among many other things, it failed to understand that true rulership is stewardship and servanthood.

This failure has continued. Ellul notes that "when the world rebelled against the West and regained its freedom, when the soldiers and the missionaries departed, the West retained its power and continued its program of exploitation, but by other means."[30]

The results of this continuance is seen everywhere in the Third World. Costly loans with all sorts of conditions and special trade agreements all favor the West. But this is not the worst form of ongoing Western domination. It is the ingrained idea that West is best and everything else is inferior.

Reflection

Domination is never simply a matter of political or economic oppression. It is also a matter of psychological onslaught that saps the roots of a healthy identity.

JULY

The Opposite

*Our best intentions with a most careful execution
can still have unintended consequences.*

That some find it hard to accept the idea that our
world is marred by sin is surprising. What kind of
optimism can blind someone so thoroughly? Sin's
havoc is everywhere. And its pernicious nature is
nowhere displayed more clearly than when it manifests itself in the aftermath of the practice of good. Ellul
writes: "How strange that the consciousness of freedom and the will to give it concrete expression
should always end in producing the opposite of what
was sought."[1]

The Greeks sought to give the world wisdom.
Much of it was folly. The Romans sought to give law
and order. Most of it was tyranny. The church sought
to bring the kingdom of God. Instead, it produced doctrines and ecclesiastical structures. Marx looked for
political and social egalitarianism. Marxism produced
an elitism and the oppression of the masses. The West
promoted freedom, but was frequently guilty of mas-
sive exploitation.

Reflection
*God needs to redeem
our best efforts.*

Shaping One's Life

Much of what we are we have received from our family and our culture. But what we finally become has everything to do with our choices.

We are created. But as Ellul rightly points out, "You create yourself by choice, by action."[2] In this, we either build on what we have received or we redirect the heritage we have received from our family and culture. Many mindlessly build on what they have. They lack a critical perception. They readily accept what has been passed on to them.

Others are not so complying. While not ungrateful for what they have received, they question their heritage. They may not be happy with its narrow-mindedness or its basic philosophy. So they wrestle with throwing off aspects of the old and struggle with creating new ways of being and acting. By making choices that do not comply with our family tradition or our cultural norms, we may be forming new social movements or institutions. But equally importantly, we will be forming a new self.

Reflection
When we fail to question what we have, we will never fully appropriate what is ours. Ultimately, we can only accept what we have embraced as our own.

Inspiration

Scripture does not only give us propositional truth. It also inspires us to be and to live differently without our clearly seeing the exact shape of what that new way of life may be.

Certain forms of Protestantism have reduced the Bible to a theological textbook. They have minimized its suggestive and emotive dimensions. The Bible contains not only the Pauline statements, but also the parables of Jesus. It contains formulas, but also dreams. It emphasizes the word, but also celebrates the power and significance of the deed. Moreover, the Bible always points us to a spiritual reality that is beyond the confines of the logic of this world.

Thus the Bible is always a frustrating book for those who wish to live the Christian life with pharisaical precision. For it always points us beyond our certainties to a life of faith and hope.

Ellul is therefore rightly skeptical that we can build our legalistic systems on Scripture. He writes: "What scripture shows has the strength and speed of a rushing torrent. We do not build with a torrent."[3]

A new listening to Scripture will always redefine our theological, ethical, and economic systems. But it will, more than that, inspire us to live a life of radical obedience to Christ.

Reflection
The living Word calls us to live beyond all our ethical and moral systems.

Limitation

In some incomprehensible way, God has linked
His divine power to human responsibility.

In some sense, God is radically and totally free. He
can do whatever seems good and is consistent with
His own nature. Yet that already poses a limitation. For
God cannot be God and violate an aspect of His being.
But God has voluntarily embraced further limitations.
As Ellul notes: "The God of biblical revelation, however, enters time and history, bears with the suffering
and sin of the race, tolerates its initiatives and limits
his own power."[4]

God is not the God of divine precision and heavenly calculation. In Christ, God has linked His concerns
with humanity. He is not remote. He has joined us in
our struggle. He has entered our vale of tears. This
remarkable involvement does not mean that God is for
whatever we do. He is sometimes stringently against
us. But either way, He joins with us. Either way, His
commitment is unshakable.

Whether He is correcting us or blessing us, God
is driven by an unfathomable love. And it is precisely
this love that limits His power for, when He should
punish, He surprisingly extends His grace.

Reflection
God's power is demonstrated in the
love He has for us in Christ.

Intelligence

While the heart may have reasons that the mind knows nothing about, faith uses rather than bypasses the mind.

The old distinctions between body and soul and mind and spirit were based on an untenable dualism. The human being is a unity rather than an amalgam of certain divisible parts. Similarly, playing off faith against the mind is based on unacceptable distinctions, for faith always involves the use of the mind.

Ellul puts it even more strongly. "Faith," he writes, "produces a renewal of intelligence."[5] He is right. For faith not only encourages us to love and worship God with our minds, but also stimulates us to begin to think God's thoughts after Him. Faith helps us to rethink the meaning of life and the purpose of our existence. Faith inspires us to make sense of the things around us, including the bizarre and difficult, in the light of God's revelation in Jesus Christ.

Thus, faith need never be an escape from the rigorous questions of the mind. Faith, instead, enlightens the mind with the wisdom of God.

Reflection
*Faith renews the mind
through the Word of God.*

Institutionalization

The problem lies not so much with the institutions we create, but with what institutions so often become.

There is little doubt that Jesus had in view a people movement that had everything to do with the kingdom of God. While Jesus formed a community of disciples, His impact was much wider. He not only addressed the crowds and ministered to their needs, but also mobilized them to be salt and light in their respective communities.

Jesus' vision was much wider than the training of His immediate disciples. He attracted the crowds and became a symbol of hope and change for them.

Sadly, as so often is the case, the people movement faded and the church emerged. Ellul makes the historical generalization that "once a movement becomes an institution, it is lost."[6] In one sense he is right for, ever since the Constantinian era, the church has valiantly tried to break out of its narrow institutional confines in order that it may impact more widely on the general community.

Reflection
A people's movement involves the notion of collusion rather than the churchly idea of separatism.

Accepted

*Every religious group develops its particular cri-
teria for judging who is acceptable. Jesus always
seems to defy our categories.*

Jesus' focus was not the religious institution. He was
not concerned with developing a theological system,
mode of worship, and the norms for religious affilia-
tion. But He did have a passion for people. And He had
a vision for the fulfillment of God's kingdom.

Jesus had iconoclastic tendencies. He had a concern for the things that mattered and a disdain for the
usual religious trappings. He saw people as trapped in
their own folly, busyness, and pursuits. He saw them
as alienated from His Father's love and weighed down
with meaningless religious obligations. And so He
reached out beyond the traditional religious confines
to touch the burdened and the hurting.

In this, Jesus exemplifies the simple truth
expressed by Ellul that "the person who is judged and
rejected by others is the one whom God accepts, loves,
and saves."[7]

Reflection

*Religious groups establish boundaries in
order to define and safeguard the faithful.
Jesus breaks through the boundaries
in order to embrace those who in their
need do not know where to turn.*

Selection

*God makes use of our work. But He carefully
selects what is usable and recoverable.*

God values our partnership. He wants us to participate in His plans for the world. These plans
have to do with reconciliation, liberation, and reconstruction. God desires that we be at peace with Him
and with each other. He wants us to be free from every
form of oppression and longs to see a new world based
on righteousness and grace. We are called to join God
in the fulfillment of this plan.

But we soon realize that there is much at stake. Not
only can we not make it happen by ourselves, but we
are often more of a hindrance than a help. As Ellul points
out, "God takes from man's work that which he will
make perfect and eternal."[8] God has to be selective. Most
often, He has to transform much of what we do.
Sometimes, He has to ignore what we have done and,
at other times, undo the damage we have perpetrated.

In spite of all of this, God continues to welcome
us on His team. He calls us to participation. And we
have only one option: gratefully to obey.

Action
*Work with God rather than for God,
but do not expect that God can
always use what you do.*

Beyond Our Limits

While we are "clever" at setting boundaries,
God "foolishly" destroys them and creates His
own open spaces.

Sadly, some Christians live as if God is under their control. They defend God, speak on His behalf, and claim to know all the latest things that God is planning to do in the church and the world. They fail to realize that God is uncontrollable. Much of what He does is unknowable.

Ellul points out that "Christians behave in all things as if the God whom they proclaim had no active reality outside themselves, their church, and their dogmas."[9]

Thankfully, neither the individual Christian, a particular church, or a particular theological perspective has all the answers. God is beyond our systems. He breaks the limits we set for Him. He reveals Himself in the streets as much as in the church. He can use the stumbling seeker after truth as much as the learned priest. He is at work in the world in ways that many pious church workers will never understand.

Reflection
Expect to meet God anywhere.
He is the God of surprises.

Reversals

Everything in life does not always turn out as
was reasonably expected. This does not neces-
sarily mean that we took a wrong course of
action. Nor does it mean that God was
unconcerned or uninvolved.

We want our world to be manageable. Therefore, it must be predictable. Certain things must follow. If good has been done, then further good must follow. If evil has been perpetrated, then justice must have its way.

But in our refractory world, things do not always turn out as expected. Not even for the Christian. Sometimes suffering and deprivation follow on the heels of our doing good. Sometimes blessings come our way when the opposite is deserved.

Ellul, in emphasizing the intractable nature of social reality, notes that "the struggle for freedom has multiplied dictators."[10] Equally, the church has often brought bigotry and the doing of good has bred dependence. The challenge in all of this is not that we drop all expectations and cease to do good. Rather, it is that we leave the results to God and strive to live in a more open and less controlling way.

Action
Act as if we are not making it all happen.
Otherwise the results will be less than good,
even though our intentions were noble. God
must redeem even our best projects.

God's Order

God's order has more to do with the practice of
love, justice, and mercy than it has to do with
the creation of systems and institutions.

Theologians have rightly emphasized that God is
responsible for the orders of creation, namely, family, work, and the state. Moreover, God instituted the
priesthood and kingship in the Old Testament and the
church in the New Testament. Thus, God's order is
expressed in certain institutional forms. The emphasis for us then becomes: Get the structures right and
we will express God's rule on earth.

But this can get us way off the mark. For the
emphasis should fall not so much on the structures
themselves, but on the quality of life these structures
are meant to reflect.

Ellul goes so far as to say that "God's order is not
organisation and institution."[11] God's order is reflected
in the practice of love, justice, and mercy, and all institutional reality must be circumscribed by this tripartite
heartbeat. If this does not occur, then our very institutions may exist to serve merely the status quo and
so eventually become oppressive.

Action
Practice the revolutionary way of
love, justice, and mercy and so
call the system to account.

Living with God

*We are sustained by God and we are called
to live in His presence.*

In some sense, we are all sustained by God whether we
acknowledge Him or not, for our very existence is due
to God's creative activity. Christians acknowledge this—
they profess that they are supported and nourished by
the grace of God and the work of His Spirit. God is the
One who upholds us. He keeps us. The Christian life is
not lived by our own strength. God empowers us. We
don't live by our own wisdom. The Spirit enlightens us.
Thus, our life is wholly dependent on God.

This does not mean that we do nothing and leave
everything to God, for the God who upholds us is the
God who calls us to live in His presence. And prayer
is one of the ways in which we can do that. Jacques
Ellul, therefore, is right when he notes that "prayer is
not discourse. It is a form of life with God."[12] It is the
way of openness. It is a means of fellowship. It is the
gateway to listen. It is a channel of grace. It is a means
of empowerment. It is the way to be with the God who
consistently loves us in Jesus Christ.

Reflection
*The prayerful person is
an empowered person.*

The Words of the Wise

*The wise are believable, not so much because of
the profundity of their utterances, but because of
the consistency of their lifestyle.*

Wisdom has little to do with the propagation of
high-sounding ideas. It has much more to do with
the promotion of practical knowledge that has stood the
test of life experience. The wise, therefore, are not simply ideas people. Instead, they are people who have
walked the dusty road and know something of the pain
of the journey as well as the contours of the road.

However, the wise cannot tell us exactly what we
should do. They are not gurus. Nor are they crystal ball
gazers. In the words of Ellul: "The word of the wise
makes us advance."[13]

The wise can encourage. They can challenge us
to take new risks. To adopt new strategies. To look at
life differently. And we listen to them not because they
mesmerize us with their charisma, but because they
carry the wounds and the victories of the journey. And
we will listen all the more closely if the wise themselves
have walked in the wisdom of the God of the sages.

Reflection
*Not to listen to the wisdom
of others is a reflection of either
our pride or our insecurity.*

Lifestyle

A just lifestyle involves not simply practical care for our brothers and sisters in Christ. It also involves care for the least of those in the general community and a commitment to change the structures that oppress them.

Ellul is emphatic that if "Christianity today may have a point of contact with the world, it is less important to have theories about economic and political questions . . . than it is to create a new style of life."[14] He is right, even though theory and practice should belong together. But if practice is lacking, our theories will not achieve much good.

So then, what should our practice display? Here are some tentative suggestions. First, we should demonstrate that the power of mammon has been broken in our life by the practice of a simple lifestyle and downward mobility.

Second, we should overcome the push toward individualism by the experience of community. This involves opening our lives and our homes to the needs and gifts of others.

Finally, we should resist the power of tradition by exploring how things could be different in the creation of a more just society.

Action
Allow the Man for Others to turn you around. So much of what we do is ultimately for ourselves.

Taking Responsibility

*Neither an impersonal fate nor equally imper-
sonal bureaucratic structures can be held
accountable for our decisions and actions.
Living before a personal God makes us personally accountable.*

To live in the sight of God is neither overwhelm-
ing nor debilitating. Instead, it is freeing. For the
God before whom we live enhances our role as
responsible beings. Rather than controlling us, He calls
us to decision. He sets out the path of life, but invites
us to walk that path obediently and to work out the
practical implications. Thus, freedom means having
the opportunity to live obediently and responsibly.

Ellul notes that to be "free means being capable
of accepting the consequences of one's words and
actions and behaviour and taking responsibility for
what one has done and been."[15] God places us in the
world as responsible agents and we cannot blame the
wickedness of the world or the Devil for our wrongdoing. However, we also cannot take pride in ourselves
for our right doing. God has given us enough light by
which to prevent wrongdoing and enough grace for
right doing.

Action
*Do good and
therefore be free.*

Caring, but Careful

God's care for us is governed by a wisdom that frequently defies our human reasoning. But it has our well-being in view.

Ellul notes that "God is not dumb, or blind, or deaf to the cry of his creatures, though he is also not an automatic dispenser of the graces and privileges and miracles that we demand."[16] God's care, therefore, is careful.

This does not mean that God's love ever holds back, for His love is boundless. We know this from the awesome display of His love in the gift of His Son. But God's love is directive. It is not sentimental do-goodism. It certainly is not giving us what we think we need. God's love and care is sustaining. It is there even when we think we don't need it. It is also intervening. God does step in when we are in desperate circumstances, although not always in the way that we would like. But most of all, God's love is personally formative. He has in view the shaping and molding of our lives so that we will express His glory and realize our full potential as creatures of His grace.

Reflection
God hears our cry, but responds according to His wisdom.

Action

Practical involvement in real life issues can easily undermine and change our theories, ideas, and theologies.

The "best" parents in the world are those who have no children. They know exactly how children should be brought up and disciplined.

For real parents, child rearing is far more difficult and ambiguous. This observation also holds for other areas of life. People who have no business experience know exactly how Christian business people should run their enterprises. And those who have never entered the "dirty" world of politics readily pontificate how Christians should act in such an arena.

In real life, things are not so easy. Nor are things so self-evident. While the "best" football players are always on the sideline, once they enter the fray of the game, they soon discover the difference between theory and practice. Ellul is clear: "You can't act without getting your hands dirty."[17]

This does not mean that one compromises basic Christian values. It simply means that, in the reality of the situation, we are less self-assured and have fewer easy answers.

Reflection
In the real situation,
we have to live by faith.

The Ultimate Gift

The radical nature of evil requires radical solutions. God's commitment to providing an answer sets the tone for our fight against evil.

Ellul reminds us that "it is because the world is radically, totally evil that nothing less would do than the gift of God's Son."[18] Blessings, warning, law, and prophet were not enough. God Himself in Christ had to enter the human arena to absorb sin's power and annul it. God Himself found the way to empower men and women to live new lives.

God's strategy in depowering evil is significant and illuminative. In Christ, all that was holy and good was clearly displayed. Consequently, all that was evil was decidedly exposed. The final folly of evil was its attempt to destroy the good, only to find itself robbed of its power. Christ triumphed over evil through the mystery of the Cross. Life triumphs in death. Victory emerges in the shame of Golgotha. God's power is displayed through weakness.

This form of ultimate giving and its triumph over evil is a model for our action in the world as we seek to proclaim to the world that the prison doors are open. Those bound by sin have been freed in Christ and can embrace that freedom through faith in Christ.

Reflection

Evil cannot triumph in the face of the demonstration of the good in Christ.

Holiness

*Starting with the initial changes that our new
relationship in Christ brings, God is gently but
persistently committed to molding our lives in
order that they may reflect His holiness.*

While holiness seems to be such an ethereal idea,
particularly in our secular and pragmatic world,
it is, nevertheless, intensely practical and relevant.
Holiness has to do with being set apart to do what God
asks of us and with reflecting His values. These two
ideas are closely related. If we really do what God
wants, then we need to do things God's way.

Yet the path to holiness is difficult for us. We frequently think that we know what is best and we most
often do things our way. Growth in holiness, therefore,
is seldom a gentle development for us. It comes to us
by way of struggle. Ellul notes that "purification is by
way of testing and suffering."[19] Often difficulty is where
we learn our lessons. In hardship our lives are molded.
In those circumstances, God not only rescues us, but
shapes new realities in our lives. Growth in holiness,
therefore, is often the path of God's discipline.

Reflection
*God's strategy is to make us more like
Himself. He will use anything
toward that end, including pain.*

The Hound of Heaven

God pursues us passionately with His grace. As a result, a person's conversion can be a most dramatic turnaround.

Some people's conversion is like the gentle awakening of the dawn. Change takes place gradually and almost imperceptibly. For them, the boundaries are not clear. They are not really sure when they moved from not knowing God to knowing Him truly. The only thing they now know is that by faith they do truly know Him.

For others, change was very different. For Ellul, "it was a very brutal and very sudden conversion."[20] He tells us little more. Clearly for some, the gentle approach does not work. God has to come with power and confrontation. This intrusion is equally a sign of God's love. God's love does not fear confrontation, but He pursues us to the end.

This may mean that one is overpowered by the light of God's truth and grace. It does not mean that one is involuntarily converted. In the midst of a powerful encounter, we can still respond negatively. But our positive response is always due to the grace of God.

Reflection
Conversion, however it occurs, is always a transition from the old to the new.

Building Christian Community

*In building Christian community, more is
required than that women and men be together.
A common way of life with a common vision for
action in the world are basic elements.*

Ellul notes that "all functional mechanisms, the
institutional nuts and bolts, the whole ideological
superstructure are just religious appearances. But
that is not church."[21]

He is right. The heavy ecclesiastical machinery
that consumes so much of the time and resources of
being church has in fact little to do with the church's
essential nature.

The church should above all else be a community,
people in relationship sharing a common life in
Christ. It involves mutual support and care not only
for the spiritual dimension of life, but for all of life.
Community, moreover, involves a "common" mission
in the world. The emphasis on "common," however,
has little to do with conformity. Community life is
focused, but not constricting. It can celebrate diversity and emphasizes freedom within the framework of
commitment and responsibility.

Action
*Build Christian community—open, vulnerable,
and sharing—that leads to friendship that
includes journeying with each other for the
long haul of life's challenges and commitments.*

Rebuilding

The task of rebuilding our communities has everything to do with participatory and empowering processes.

There is much good in our world. Everywhere there are men and women of goodwill and families and communities of peace and justice. But there is also a lot that is wrong in our world. Discrimination, injustice, and oppression characterize many communities and entire societies. The call to be salt, leaven, and light in our world and to see the lordship of Christ expressed in every area of life poses a great challenge for every Christian.

In responding to this challenge, Christians must avoid simplistic answers and one-sided strategies. Ellul notes that in "confronting social ills and immorality, the masculine mind finds only the one solution: that of making laws and setting up rules and sanctions."[22]

More permanent changes are achieved by participatory rather than top-down strategies. Moreover, participatory strategies always have a pastoral dimension.

Reflection
*Empowerment involves
the art of nurture.*

Person or Principle?

*Patterning our lives on the words and deeds of
Jesus will always lead to a more radical
approach to life than to pattern our lives on
broad moral principles.*

Closely associating with Jesus is always a dangerous business, for Jesus managed to be out of step
with His contemporaries. He didn't side with the
Jewish religious establishment or the ascetic Qumran
communitarians, or the radical, political Zealots, or
with the Roman authorities. Jesus had His own vision
as to how life should be lived.

This vision had everything to do with God's rule
expressed by the values of reconciliation, peace, and
justice. Jesus preached good news. Healed the sick.
Cast out demons. Mobilized the masses. Gave hope to
the poor. Built Christian community. And defiantly
resisted oppressive religious laws.

To live like this is also dangerous business for us.
But it is more effective than to live only by broad
Christian principles that, while right, fail to put us at
the cutting edge of human need and social change.

Reflection

*"We cannot dream of reducing Christianity
to a certain number of principles,"
notes Ellul, because the person of
Christ "is the principle of everything."*[23]

The Present Tense

*Facing the present and all its challenges and
possibilities makes for a lifestyle that is
purposive and hopeful.*

We carry the past with us. Our experience of our family of origin is in us. Our experience of schools,
friends, the workplace, and the general community is very
much with us. All of this has left an indelible mark.

But we are also much more than all of these
things. We have our own unique personality. We have
absorbed and adapted to particular influences in particular ways. More specifically, our own God-given
creativity has enabled us to respond to the challenges
and opportunities that have come our way. Ellul's
advice, therefore, is pertinent: "We must live in the
present. We must not escape into memories of the past
or into some glorious future."[24]

This does not mean that our past is unimportant
or that we should not face the future with hope. It simply means that we need to face the present realistically
and purposefully.

Reflection
*Opportunities missed in the
present seldom return.*

Silence

*The gift of silence is a necessary prerequisite for
the experience of reflection and meditation. But
silence should still involve presence.*

The constant risk for all of us is that we overcrowd our
lives. Pushed by inner compulsions, self-imposed
demands, and the pressures of our busy schedules, we
fail to create spaces for silence and reflection.
Consequently, we are often devoid of inner resources,
fresh ideas, and creativity. We manage as best we can, sustained by our past experiences and expertise.

A healthy rhythm of life, however, involves the
act of disengagement. We need times to be still. To pray.
To reflect. So that we can be renewed.

While stillness involves silence, it is not without
presence. In stillness we need to know that God is with
us. Ellul notes that "in the silence and absence of God
we are truly orphans."[25] But meditation should not lead
to such an experience. Instead, in silence we need to
be embraced by the God who welcomes us.

Reflection
*Stillness is shutting off the
human voices so that the voice
of God may be clearly heard.*

Harmony

Harmony involves the bringing together of disparate elements. It has nothing to do with uniformity.

Both our physical and social worlds are wondrously diverse. And diversity is beautiful if its uniqueness is appreciated and celebrated. Diversity is all the more significant if its possibilities for complementarity are utilized.

This involves bringing things together. Joining without destroying. Fusing without obliterating. All this has to do with harmony.

But, as Ellul so perceptively points out, "when stability is achieved there is no more harmony."[26] For harmony seldom means final resolution. Instead, harmony is cooperation in the midst of differentness. Such an understanding of harmony should characterize our families, churches, and community organizations. Far too often we settle for domination and uniformity. This is so, because frequently this is easier to achieve.

The royal road of harmony is far more difficult. But it also more fully reflects God's intention for His creatures.

Action

Create harmony by using skills that lead all to participate in a commonly articulated vision.

Humility

Humility is not self-negation. It is a knowing and acting based upon an acceptance of our finiteness.

While many may never dream any dreams of grandeur, there are always those who strongly believe in their abilities and their place in the world—so much so that they believe they can make their mark on history and make the world a better place.

The rhythm of successive years, however, tends to erode such naked optimism. An individual's contribution is seen increasingly for what it is—a mere drop in a bucket. And the march of history inexorably continues with little change in sight despite one's best efforts to effect change.

None of this should persuade us to become inactive. It merely encourages us to be more realistic and humble. Ellul points out: "It is precisely the wise man who knows that he is not wise."[27] Similarly, it is the activist who realizes that only little can be achieved. Being humble need not decrease our commitment. It will, however, increase our focus on prayer and joining hands with others.

Action
Show humility by welcoming another's part in the overall mission.

Political Allegiance

In our modern world, Christians have tended to
support the political parties of the traditional
Right, even though their agenda so often lacks
God's passion for justice.

God's concern for justice is expressed everywhere in
the pages of Scripture. God hates oppression. He
despises faulty weights and measures. He thoroughly
disapproves of exploitation. He is concerned about the
poor and needy.

Sadly many churches, particularly in the West,
have lost touch with the poor and aligned themselves
with conservative politics, what Ellul sees as parties
of the political Right. Ellul hoists his flag: "I have nothing to say for or about the Right because I have no
common standard with it. I am a stranger to it."[28] Not
that the so-called Left has all the answers, either. The
issue instead is that Christians should emulate God's
passion for justice. In walking this road, they may not
find much common cause with the Right or Left. In
fact, their stance will be more radical than either group.

Reflection
If we lack a passion for justice, we have
probably succumbed to a political ethic
that is not aligned with the needy.

Life's Rhythm

Life is not only a series of choices. It also has a perceptible rhythm, the "laws" of which one needs to obey.

We are aware of the biological rhythm that leads from birth to death. Sociologically, we also experience certain patterns of social life. And spiritually we speak of the seasons of the inner life. Life is, therefore, more than the decisions we make. It also has an identifiable pattern.

This does not mean that we are irrevocably bound to certain psychological or sociological laws. But it does mean that we need to understand our family background, the way we best operate, and the social factors that impinge themselves upon our lives. In other words, we are never without certain external constraints and certain inner motivations. Instead of always trying to work against these factors, we need to learn to work within them. As Ellul notes, "Things have a rhythm of their own and, if you want them done well, you have to respect it, without imposing solutions from outside."[29]

Reflection
To go with the flow is not such a bad idea when it relates to respecting the way we are made and the way in which we best function.

A Changed Church

While the church is ever ready to pontificate as to how the rest of society should order itself, it frequently fails to clean up the mess in its own backyard.

It is quite right that the church should have something to say to the rest of the world, because the church does not exist simply for the sake of heaven, but also for the sake of the world. The desire to be relevant is not the problem. But the failure to practice what the church preaches is.

The church cannot only be a word to the world. It must also be a model. Its word to the world must first become flesh in the Christian community. This is not to say that the church must first be perfect before it can bring a challenge to the world. But there must be a substantial reality. The church must be wrestling with the issues. It must demonstrate some reality. Therefore, Ellul can rightly assert that "the church would have to be changed in order to become a leaven, a force to change society."[30]

Action
*Change yourself before
seeking to change others.*

Different, Not Isolated

In the desire of Christians to not do as the world does, they need to be careful that they do not separate themselves from the very men and women and situations that they are seeking to influence.

Christians often live between a rock and a hard place. They want to respond to the biblical injunction not to be like the world. On the other hand, they also want to respond in love to their neighbor, including the neighbor who is outside of the Christian faith. And because love knows how to walk the second mile and is committed to getting its hands dirty in serving that neighbor, love's strategy is more about joining than about separation.

Ellul also highlights the tension in which Christians find themselves. "Christians ought to try to create a style of life which does not differentiate them from others, but yet permits them to escape from the stifling pressure of our present form of civilization."[31] This means that Christians need to be involved in the world without being worldly. They need to respond to the world without accepting its agenda.

Reflection
*"Engaged but different" should epitomize
the Christian's role in the world.*

AUGUST

The Praying Heart

Prayer can be so much more than the specific acts of prayer. It can be the very heartbeat of our life.

Christians are regularly called on to pray. Mealtimes. Church services. Special meetings. The list could go on. This in itself is not a problem. To pray at many occasions is fine. The problem is that much of this kind of praying can become trite and superficial. Ellul says that such public prayers "are covering prayers, putting us right with God at the opening of the session; then, since we have called upon him, we feel all the more free not to take the Lord into account during the course of the discussions."[1]

Clearly, this kind of praying will not be effective. Something else needs to come in its place. It is the praying heart that should characterize us. It is constantly looking to God for His participation, grace, and blessing, no matter what we are doing. It is praying when we are not praying. It is a constant communion. It is a cry or whisper of the heart. It is a reaching out to God even in the midst of our busyness.

Reflection

*Prayer is always more than saying
formal prayers. Prayer is
touching the divine.*

The Power of a Life

*While an individual may not be able to change
the world, a person with moral integrity cannot
but make an impact.*

Every Christian grapples with the question: How can
I make my life useful? This question arises from
the belief that we are not to live only for ourselves. We
are to live to God's glory by living according to His
Word. And this Word calls us to serve our neighbor.
So we grapple with the question whether we should
serve God in some formal ministry or serve Him in the
workplace. We juggle family and work responsibilities
with our desire to serve God in a wider arena. No one
can escape these questions and struggles.

What we must escape, however, is the temptation
to try to do too much. There is little virtue in blessing
others while we destroy our own family life. We need
to recognize that we can only do so much. The most
important thing is the quality of what we do rather than
the quantity. Since quality has everything to do with
character and integrity, the issue is not simply what we
are doing, but how God is forming and shaping us.

Reflection
*"The most useful thing a Christian can
do is to live, and life understood from the
point of view of faith has an extraordinary,
explosive force," writes Ellul.[2]*

Radical Change

*The vision of the kingdom of God is always
subversive, for it envisages a change from the
old order to the new.*

Ellul confides that "the issue of revolution . . . has
remained central to my life."[3] This may initially
strike us as strange. Revolution is more the province
of social activists than theologians.

But radical change, the key factor in any revolution, lies at the very heart of the biblical message. We
believe in the need for the radical change of individuals through faith in Jesus Christ. We also believe that
our communities should be touched by the redemptive and transforming grace of Christ. Moreover, we
believe that our societies and their social, economic,
and political structures should be tempered by the values of God's kingdom. No area of life should remain
untouched by the changing power that flows from the
Cross of Christ. Therefore, radical language that has
become the sole province of parties of the traditional
Left should be reappropriated by the Christian community as it seeks to work out a practical expression
of Christianity governed by love and justice.

Action
*Live by the grace of
God and act justly.*

Earthkeepers

God has given us great responsibility in making us vice-regents under His lordship. In this, He treats us as mature sons and daughters rather than as dependent children.

We cannot do with our personal lives whatever we wish, because we have a responsibility to give God an account for the things we have done. Similarly, we have a responsibility for what we do to this world. Ellul writes: "Humankind is responsible for—that is, they will have to answer to God for—what happens on earth."[4]

While we may say that the big picture is not directly within our sphere of responsibility, we do play a part. We can contribute to building a form of community that overcomes alienation. We can contribute to peaceful processes that defuse aggression and violence. We can promote a justice that negates oppression. We can live a simple lifestyle that promotes responsible stewardship. Moreover, we can support policies and projects that demonstrate care for our fragile environment.

Action

Live responsibly and do the little you can. But also join with others so that you can do the seemingly impossible.

Self-Criticism

*No one is so blind as the person who is
incapable of self-criticism.*

It is not difficult for us to see faults in others. Nor is
it difficult for us to operate on the basis that we are
right at least most of the time. But in our need to be
right we can also become somewhat blinded. For we
often so much need to be right that we can begin to
justify everything. Ellul notes that we can come to the
point where "excusing everything in our party, our
friends and our allies," we only reserve "moral criticism for our enemies."[5]

The problem here is not that we should be blind
to the faults of others. Rather, we should first of all engage
ourselves in rigid self-reflection. If we don't, we will not
only stifle personal growth and development, but we may
also project some of our issues onto others. Christian
morality suggests that we should be hard on ourselves
in terms of self-criticism and easy on others.

Reflection
*Self-criticism is not to be a guilt-driven
negative pursuit. Instead, it is to be a positive
reflection on our strengths and weaknesses.*

Knowledge of Good and Evil

If we want to do what is good, we need to discern what is evil.

The primal innocence of the Garden of Eden is no longer characteristic of our lives. We now live in a difficult state of affairs. Both the natural knowledge and the ability to do ultimate good is lost to us. What good is has become a shadowy reality.

But this is not our only problem. We are now also confused about the nature of evil. In fact, we sometimes call evil good and, under the guise of doing what is right, we perpetrate further wrongdoing. Ellul observes that the average human being "has even less knowledge of the true [nature of] evil than he has of the good."[6] That we need to discern what is evil in order that we may know and do what is good is an important given for Christian living and action. Such discernment cannot come from ourselves. We need God's light from His Word to expose the nature of evil and we need God's empowerment to do what is good.

Reflection

*What is evil or good frequently defies
the neat boundaries we create. The church
is frequently neither wholly good nor is
the world wholly evil in the sense that
we cannot learn anything from it.*

Peacemakers

We have been called and redeemed by the Prince
of Peace, but we easily follow the gods of war.

The dangerous memory in early Christianity was
that an innocent man who proclaimed the kingdom of God and went about doing good suffered a
cruel and violent death at the hands of the religious
and political establishments. This man Jesus made no
attempt to justify or to protect Himself. He certainly
did nothing to retaliate. It is this Jesus whom we
acknowledge as Lord and Savior and who calls us to
live His kind of life in today's world.

Yet it is precisely on this point that we find it so
difficult to follow Jesus. Everything within us seems
to cry out for the right to justify ourselves. To protect
ourselves. To retaliate. And the church's history is full
of such retaliation. It is a history of the sword wielded
in the name of religion much more than a history of
the peaceful dove. Ellul is right when he writes that
"violence seems to be the great temptation in the
church and among Christians today."[7]

Reflection
To be a peacemaker requires more creativity
and courage than to be a warmonger.

Pierced to the Heart

The powerful impulse in the West is to celebrate an uninhibited eros, a proud individualism, and unhindered progress. But the gospel constantly calls Western values into question.

There are two forces that have shaped the West. These can be represented in any one of these three ways: as Athens and Jerusalem, as the Renaissance and the Reformation, or as secular humanism and the Christian faith. Ellul typifies these forces as Greek *eros* or sexual love, on the one hand, and Christian *agape* or altruistic love, on the other.

Throughout the West's long history, the one or the other has been dominant. In our modern era, eros predominates rather than agape. Humanism rather than Christianity. Rationalism rather than spirituality. Progress rather than stewardship. But humanism, rationalism, and unhindered progress cannot triumph. Ellul points out that "the West has never been able to reach its logical end because it was pierced to the heart by a gospel that was its utter opposite."[8] The gospel of Christ is the powerful antidote. It calls into question all of our proud pretensions and calls us to bow the knee before the God who loves and redeems us.

Reflection
We need to make the gospel relevant. But the worst thing we can do is to change it and thereby strip it of its power.

What Sort of Power?

*To a greater or lesser degree, we all exercise
some form of power. But the question of power
must be linked to the issue of morality.*

We are all familiar with the notion of positional
power, where people exercise responsibility by
virtue of the office they hold. We also know the impact
that moral power can have. This is power exercised on
the basis of integrity and the vision of what is good.
Both of these expressions of power can be good.

But we have also experienced the wrong use of
power, particularly that which is manipulative and
exploitative. Ellul, however, probes the theological
dimension of power and claims that "man's power is
first of all the result of hardening his heart against
God."[9] He is right. Human beings by nature are in
opposition to God and in flight from Him. Therefore,
what we do is motivated by self-justification. It is only
by inner transformation that we can come to the place
where our exercise of power is motivated by service
to God rather than service of self.

Reflection
*The power that serves is the
power that empowers.*

Crossing Deserts

*The desert remains a fundamental feature
in everyone's spiritual journey.*

Conversion does not bring us from the desert into the Promised Land. The reverse is true. It is the converted who actually become candidates for the desert. The unconverted have no interest in the desert. They avoid such places. They are only too happy to live in the normal world. The converted don't enjoy the desert either. In fact, they live in the vain hope that they can bypass the desert.

But this is not possible. Ellul notes that "in our earthly lives we are still called individually, as a church and collectively to cross spiritual deserts."[10] We cannot avoid times of testing and temptation. Nor can we avoid the need for purging. And there will always be periods in our spiritual journey where we feel alone and forsaken. There are for all of us times when the voice of God seems to have lapsed into silence and when the heavens seem to be as brass.

While such times appear to be our worst moments, they are usually the heralds of the dawning of a new day.

Reflection
*In the desert, God works with us in
new and often incomprehensible ways.*

Listening

*Our conversation with the people of our time
would be deeper if we first listened more
carefully to the wisdom of God.*

Christians have a lot to say. But much of their conversation is in-house. They are busy splitting
theological hairs and defending denominational priorities. Ellul rebukes them with the observation that
"any time we read the Bible to find arguments or jus-
tifications, we wallow in Christian ideology."[11]

Clearly, we need to read Scripture in a different
way. The Bible is not a book of proof texts for our
favored position. It is God's explosive book that will
always challenge our ideas and dynamite our ideologies. Consequently, we need to learn new ways of
listening. And one of the more important strategies is
to learn to hear things that are against ourselves. This
means that we need to hold our positions as presuppositions rather than as finalities. In this way we can
be led deeper in our understanding of God's wisdom.

Reflection
*For those who think that they already
know, listening is a tiresome process.*

Walking Alone

*While partnership is an important theme in
Christian spirituality, there are times when one
must walk alone.*

There is nothing virtuous about always being in step
with everyone else, just as there is nothing virtuous in being out of step for no other reason than just
to appear to be different. But there are times when we
must walk alone. Ellul observes that "once you have
acquired a certain knowledge and experience, you
must walk alone."[12]

Sometimes, we walk alone because life experiences have given us a certain wisdom that others may
not yet possess. At other times, we walk alone because
we are experiencing pressures and difficulties that others do not understand. But more frequently, we walk
alone because we are called to walk a particular journey and fulfill a particular ministry. While we should
accept this solitary dimension of our journey, we
should never idealize it, for most frequently we are to
walk with others.

Reflection
*To walk alone does not mean
that God is absent.*

The Acts Community

While Christians hold that all the doctrines of the Bible are to be appropriated in the name of Christ, they are generally less comfortable with practices of the Bible.

Those of us who are Christians are adamant that belief should shape our conduct. We maintain that we should live a distinctive lifestyle that sets us apart from others who do not acknowledge the lordship of Christ in their lives. Yet we are uncomfortable with the distinctives of the Acts community. Sharing our resources, goods, and property because we are brothers and sisters in Christ seems much too radical to us.

And yet it is an option we should consider, particularly in a world where faith has become such a privatized and internalized reality. We urgently need to find more concrete models by which we express our faith in Christ so that the world may see that the Christian life contains a radical practical expression. Ellul is sure that "we may live truly by the Spirit in a community like that described in Acts."[13] He is right. It only takes great courage and commitment to live a new economic reality.

Action
We are good at charity. Take the extra step of modeling structural justice.

Opposing Forces

*When everything seems to be moving in the
right direction, some hindrance will thwart
the process.*

The Cross of Christ demonstrates that there is no
smooth evolutionary process leading to victory and
success. The Jesus movement had hardly begun to
mobilize the people when opposition appeared from the
religious establishment. And that very opposition
finally "won" the day at Golgotha. The surprise is not
that the religious establishment "won," but that Christ
rose from the dead.

Thus victory is not a historical process, but an irrup-
tion. Ellul notes that "in society no force has ever been
at work without giving rise to a counterforce."[14] Forces
for good are soon overtaken by reactionary elements. The
fight for justice soon gets thwarted by those who have
too much to lose. But good can and does triumph. When
it does, it is always a miracle. While our hard work and
our prayers may have contributed, of themselves these
means cannot ensure success. The triumph of good is
nothing other than the triumph of God's grace.

Reflection
*Only God can make
apparent failure triumph.*

Perseverance

*The person who continues the journey despite
the odds is one who has clearly understood his
or her calling.*

There is absolutely no reason to suggest that a
Christian's life cannot be successful. For after all,
God has promised to be with us and bless us in all we
do. The issue, rather, lies in our definition of success.
And at the very heart of the biblical idea of success lies
the notion of faithfulness. The successful life is the obedient life. And this involves perseverance.

Ellul remarks that a person "must play his part
in the life of the church and be prepared to carry on,
whether or not there is any tangible proof of results."[15]
This is equally true of our role in the world. We need
to be committed to more than just quick results.
Instead, we need a vision for laying good foundations
and in small ways modeling what a changed world
would look like.

Action
*Persevere and be courageous in being
a signpost of the kingdom of God.*

Revolutionary Action

*The greatest form of revolutionary change is not
to pull down the old. It is to create the new.*

The use of radical language has been lost to the
church. Such language has become the sole
province of those to the left of the political spectrum.
However, both radical language and action needs to be
restored to the church, for the church can never be the
mere supporter of the status quo. Because the church's
final vision is based upon a new heaven and new earth
characterized by righteousness, the present calling is
to demonstrate the embryonic form of the new world.

Ellul remarks that the Christian, by making "the
coming of the kingdom actual, is a true revolutionary."[16] For the kingdom of God does not reflect the
values of this age. Nor is it premised on worldly priorities. Nor does it build our political and economic
systems. Instead, the kingdom of God is the great dis-
turber in our world. It is the action of God that subverts
our proud achievements. It is the presence of God's
grace, peace, and justice in a world that finally man-
ages to pervert its own good.

Action
*Live the values of the kingdom and lay
the ax at the root of the old order.*

Self-Criticism

*A lack of self-criticism usually means a
lack of mature self-development.*

We are not talking about morbid introspection. Nor are we talking about a fragile individual who constantly looks inward in order to find a basis for hope and security. Nor are we discussing a perfectionist personality that constantly measures the inner spiritual barometer. We are simply referring to the need to be self-critical.

Ellul notes that "there is no freedom without an accompanying critical attitude to the self."[17] In order for self-criticism to be constructive, it must be based on a love, rather than on a rejection of the self. Its impulse must be toward a greater holism. And its fundamental starting point has to do with wanting to live in greater conformity to the will of God. Thus, both Word and Spirit can be powerful aids in our self-reflection. But learning from what we do and how we operate is also helpful. A final point is that we need to be open to the feedback of trusted friends who sometimes can see far more clearly how we need to change than we ourselves can.

Reflection
*Self-reflection is the starting
point to repentance.*

Beyond Words

The cry of the heart is deeper than what words can express.

An incessant desire. A persistent dream. A longing hope. A partial vision. A vague hunch. These all belong to the art of prayer. The cry of despair. The sigh of hopelessness. Tears of grief. The pain of loss. These are also the language of prayer. Moments of insight. Times of ecstasy. Inspiration. Empowerment. These are also part of the prayer life. In fact, so much belongs to the realm of prayer. If we are a praying people and believe that our connectedness to God is an essential part of our spirituality, then prayer should include all of our life's concerns.

But such prayer is often beyond words. As Ellul rightly observes: "Prayer . . . largely overflows the confines of the spoken language."[18] It is often the sigh of helplessness or a cry of the heart. It is our inner self joining with the Spirit of God to express things that our minds have not yet fully articulated.

Reflection
*It matters most to whom you pray.
It matters little how you pray. It
matters a lot that you pray.*

Doers

*The ancient Greeks celebrated philosophical
speculation and denigrated manual labor.
Christians must make sure that they do not
follow in their footsteps and exalt thinking
over doing.*

Ellul castigates the "intelligentsia who live on a diet
of words in doing nothing."[19] This can also be a
problem for the Christian community. We hear endless sermons. We have attended multiple training
courses and specialized programs. Yet we often don't
feel adequate for the task and remain immobilized.

A key problem lies in our educational method-
ology. Direct knowledge transfer from the expert
trainer to the largely passive learner is hardly a good
way to equip people for action. We learn better by
doing, particularly when the doing is monitored by a
mentor who provides both guidance and evaluation.
But there are other difficulties as well. Action always
involves risk and risk brings with it uncertainty. We
therefore need to face our own basic insecurities.
Because we can never be wholly sure that our actions
will be productive or appreciated, we need to learn to
act in faith and hope rather than wait until we can fully
predict the outcome.

Reflection
*Action involves planning. It also
involves overcoming our fears.*

Free to Be Servants

*To be empowered to live a life pleasing to
God is the highest form of freedom.*

L et us not fool ourselves. We cannot easily achieve
God's best. In fact, we frequently do not carry out
our own best intentions. This is because lack of consistency and resolve get in the way. More particularly,
we sometimes feel quite powerless to carry out what
we know we should. Ellul reminds us that "God's
people are set free only to be placed under God's control."[20] In order to be able to do that which pleases God,
we need to be freed and empowered.

This experience of freedom involves not only freedom from the power of sin, which undermines the
moral fabric of our lives. It also involves freedom from
our own "good" ideas and plans. However, freedom
must lead to empowerment. We need inspiration, wisdom, encouragement, and perseverance. It is one thing
to have the ability to act. It is another to outwork the
commitment. It is one thing to know what to do. It is
another to have the courage to do it.

Reflection
*Christ frees us from sin. The
Spirit empowers us for action.*

Evil's Seductive Power

*If evil only appeared in evil places, then evil
could be readily identified. Unfortunately, evil
also appears where only the good is expected.*

There is nothing as perverse and debilitating as that
a place of safety becomes a place of threat and a
place of justice becomes a place of evil-doing. If a family becomes the setting for sexual abuse and the court
becomes the seat of injustice, then evil triumphs with
its seductive power. It appears where it should not be.
As Ellul points out: "Evil reigns precisely in the places
of human justice."[21]

This calls for a greater vigilance on our part. If evil
appears in good places, then we must be careful that
we do not unwittingly perpetuate evil. Good institutions can promote structural injustice when they
provide goods and services for the elite and exclude
the needy from participating.

Reflection

*It is neither wise nor true to divide the world
into a simplistic schema of "goodies" and
"baddies." Evil is far more seductive than that.*

Grace Alone

*God's grace does not create dependence. It
brings freedom and empowerment.*

The grace of God strikes us at our most vulnerable
point. This is not at our humanity. Nor is it at our
dignity. Instead, it strikes us at the point of our pride.
For at our very core we want to achieve things for ourselves. This includes our salvation.

But as Ellul points out, "No sacrifice, ceremony,
rite, or prayer can earn grace."[22] Salvation does not
come as a result of our own doing. Not even our religious much-doing. It comes as God's free gift. It comes
as freedom for the burdened. Peace for those in turmoil. Reconciliation for the alienated. Forgiveness for
the guilty. And it comes as God's gracious gift of life
for those living in the midst of death. This gift is readily grasped by those in need. It is often resisted by those
who think they already have everything. But it is freely
extended to all.

Reflection
*If salvation came by works, God would not
be impartial. He would, in fact, favor
those with resources. God's grace places
all at the same starting point.*

True Power

*God's power is freely given. But it is only given
to fulfill the will of God.*

Spurious forms of power are not strangers to the
church. We are probably most familiar with the use,
and at times the abuse, of positional power. We also
know something of the use and consequences of personality power where we are swayed by clever words
and slick performances.

But genuine power comes from the Spirit. And,
as Ellul carefully points out, "The Holy Spirit will give
true power and efficacy only to means which are in
exact agreement with the actual content of the
gospel."[23] Even the Spirit is bound by the Word. So
must we be. And we only possess true spiritual power
when what we say and do reflects God's will and therefore is graced by His blessing and power. Anything less
than that is soul power, which may be temporarily
impressive, but yields no lasting fruit.

Reflection
*The exercise of true power never
exploits. It only empowers others.*

In Our Footsteps

*No generation is without moral responsibility
to the generation that follows.*

Social scientists have made much of the process of socialization whereby the new generation is schooled in the values of the present generation. There is much truth in the observation that, in order to achieve cultural integration, a society will seek to mold its citizens into its dominant values.

But this is no ironclad law. Ellul reminds us that "the generation that comes may adopt some things from the preceding generation, but it may also reject everything and begin its own history."[24] The counter-culture youth movement of the late 1960s and early 1970s is one example.

Whether significant lasting change occurred is a moot point. The more important point is that the attempt was made, because many young people felt that they could no longer identify with society's central values. The relevance in all of this is that, while we may have things to pass on to the young, we should also train the young to be critical and experimental. They need to do better than what we have done if this world is to become a better place.

Reflection
*The best that we may pass on to the next
generation is the willingness to
dream and implement new dreams.*

Radically Different

*The challenge for Christians is not only to live
the high ground of personal morality, but also to
find radically new ways to build community and
to advocate justice.*

Ellul is stating the obvious when he observes that "if
we simply do as the world does, we can expect no
thanks, for we are doing nothing out of the ordinary."[25]

The pressing question is how can we live differently. At the most fundamental level, we are different
in belief. We acknowledge Jesus Christ as Savior and
Lord. We are also to be different in lifestyle. This difference is based on personal morality. Truthfulness and
fairness should characterize our lives. But it should not
stop here. Christians are to express God's radical saving concern for this world. This concern is to bring into
being what the Hebrew calls *shalom*: reconciliation and
a whole new set of values that demonstrate concern
for the weak and build structures of justice at the very
center of our deeply fallen world.

Action
*As you have gained everything in Christ,
risk everything in serving Him in a
world needing radical reconstruction.*

Hope

While hope can be based on mere wishful thinking that things may get better, Christian hope is based on the God who is ahead of us.

The modern person has relegated God to the past. God is part of the old mythological world, which has been replaced by the modern world of rationality and science. At least, this is what some would have us believe! But the great I Am is not so easily dismissed, and modern rationality has not replaced the human hunger for meaning and transcendence.

Rather than seeing God as essential only to a hoary past, we need to see Him as intrinsic to our future. He is already ahead of us. As the One who has made us and spans the ages in an effortless leap, God is waiting for us and beckons us forward. This call is not an invitation to return to the safe and predictable world of yesteryear. Instead, it is an invitation to shape the world that is emerging so that it may become a world of peace and justice.

Reflection
"Hope draws the future into the present," writes Ellul.[26]

The Role of the Laity

*The laity is not only not a second class in the
Christian community: It is the vehicle by which
the good news of the gospel is brought to
the world.*

Sadly, the subsequent development of the community
that Jesus founded on the basis of a servant leadership has not been without its hierarchies and social
distinctions. Traditionally, women have been treated as
second-class citizens. And the unfortunate clergy-
laity distinction has continued right up to the present.

Yet the role of the laity is critical to the building
of God's kingdom. Ellul emphasizes that the channel
through which the gospel should reach the world is
through the "layman."[27] For while clergy serve within
the structures of the church, the laity work in the
world. They are in the world as teachers, those with
family responsibilities, plumbers, doctors, and contract
workers. They are in the world pursuing their many
and varied occupations. Yet they are also there as the
people of God. The purpose of the clergy should not
be to make the plumber into a clergyperson, but to
make him or her into an effective model of Christian
witness and service in the workplace.

Reflection
*The role of the clergy is to empower the
laity to be salt and light in the world.*

The Call to Prayer

*While prayer should be as natural as breathing,
it is, instead, a commitment that we need to
make continually.*

Prayer should be easy. But most of us find it difficult. Prayer should be a great joy. But most of us
find it to be a demanding discipline. Sadly, many of us
in the West have become committed to a pragmatic
approach to life, which has robbed us of the act of
reflection, the power of meditation, and the significance of prayer. Ellul makes the pertinent observation
that "if the Christian no longer prays . . . it is because
he is completely imbued with the realism of the spirit
of the times."[28]

The praying person, therefore, is one who is out
of step with the tenor of the times. Such a person is
essentially courageous and seemingly unpractical. Yet
we urgently need such people. For praying people alone
are the ones who can hear important and insightful
things from God that have relevance for our world.

Reflection
*Prayer is a way of creating distance
between ourselves and the world so that
we hear from God anew regarding
His concerns for our world.*

Forgetting

*There are many things that should be
remembered and celebrated. These are the good
things from God's beneficent hand. Other things
should be forgotten, particularly the sins of
others against us.*

Many of us have long memories. We can readily
remember what others have said and done to us.
Sadly, we often only remember the bad things. All that
was good has faded from view. A reservoir of painful
memories is not a refreshing river in which to bathe.
It is hardly a rich resource for the long journey of life.
While future hope can empower, past well-being and
thankfulness are equally important to sustain life's forward momentum.

Ellul's observation that "forgiving and forgetting go
together"[29] is a relevant insight. It is only when we forgive and forget that we lighten the boat by jettisoning
what will always impede the journey. If we truly forgive
we will forget possibly not the deed, but the painful memory of it. And it is the painful memory, particularly when
it begins to fester, that undermines our own well-being.

Reflection
*We can never guarantee that life
will only bring us good experiences. But
we can ensure that we are not dominated
by negativity and unforgiveness.*

Self-Contradictory

No amount of faith and prayer can take away the fact that life is puzzling, self-contradictory, and less than fair.

This statement may be puzzling to some readers. They believe that faith in Christ has taken away the contradictions, and to claim that they are still there is to undermine the work of Christ in the life of a believer. However, in no way do I wish to minimize the work of Christ. His work is sufficient and transformative. But being a Christian does not take away the contradictions. In fact, it usually accents them.

Ellul comments that "human existence is essentially self-contradictory."[30] This is no less true for the believer. The believer knows the God of power, but also experiences powerlessness; knows hope, but also experiences despair; knows grace, but also falls into legalism; and has answers, but also wallows in uncertainty. The believer struggles with why the "not yet" is not fully present and why the God of providence seems so absent and removed from the pain of this world.

Reflection
Final certainty is denied until the end of this age.

No Ready-Made Answers

In our quest for ready-made answers from experts in every sphere of life, we have forgotten how to grapple with the issues for ourselves and to learn from our own life experiences.

Only a fool would suggest that we do not need experts in our complex world. But experts are only human beings with particular skills. A heart surgeon may be skillful in giving you a triple bypass operation, but may have little understanding about the broader meaning and purpose of life. The big issues of life are always the meaning issues and with these we need to grapple. There are no ready-made answers.

Ellul admits, "I never looked for anyone to explain anything to me. I worked on the problem until I could explain it to myself."[31] While at first glance this may appear to be a very arrogant approach to life, it need not be so. It can be a statement reflecting our need to struggle with the issues for ourselves. We need to make sense of our own lives. We need to come to positions on issues, having done our own homework rather than grabbing easy answers off the shelves.

Action
While we should learn from those with greater wisdom and life experience, we should finally come to our own understanding.

SEPTEMBER

Rest

Life is a rhythm of work and rest, engagement
and withdrawal, action and reflection.

The virtue of the Protestant work ethic is that it made all work "sacred," not only the work in the church sphere. The less beneficent aftermath of this ethic is that it reduced human beings to the role of worker. In this, it is not all that far removed from communist ideology, which also celebrates the person as worker.

The biblical picture is much more fully rounded. While emphasizing our role as vice-regents under God for the responsible development and shaping of our world, the Bible also knows the significance of rest and celebration. Ellul points out that "the sabbath is a gift of God to remind us that we are not constantly under the burden of . . . toil."[1] However, it is not only rest, but also celebration that rounds out the picture. Both the enjoyment of the fruit of our hands and thankful generosity, which draws our neighbor into our blessings, are part of the rhythm of life.

Reflection
Renewal comes from both
rest and celebration.

What Have We Built?

Under the guise of building a better world, we have constructed a world of greater controls and injustice.

If there is anything that characterizes the contemporary world, it is the loss of the role and significance of the individual. This is true even though more than ever before the value of the individual has been enshrined in international human rights charters. But the priority of our age has to do with corporate realities, economic priorities, the national good, and institutional concerns. Individuals exist to serve the greater good. Even the church, which fundamentally understands itself as the pilgrim people of God, is characterized by institutional concerns rather than a sense of peoplehood.

Ellul comments that "as a result of having built a world of power, man has eroded himself."[2] We create structures in the name of freedom, only to find ourselves increasingly entangled. Human beings have become means unto certain ends, which has undermined our dignity and well-being.

Reflection

If our modern cities are any reflection of what we are capable of building, then they highlight that we have created two societies, the haves and the have-nots.

New Communities

If churches do not build new communities of
hope and justice, the same tired solutions from
the elite will offer only fleeting answers, but no
significant change.

History yields a simple but painful lesson—significant change that will empower the poor and
disenfranchised will not readily come from those firmly
seated in the centers of power. It will have to come
from somewhere else. It will have to come from among
the disenfranchised themselves.

This has occurred in many Latin American countries and elsewhere in the developing world. There, the
former church of the establishment has become the
church of the poor. In the formation of base ecclesial
communities, the church has incarnated itself among
the poor. These communities have become signs of
hope. They demonstrate not only a Bible-centered spirituality, but also practical care, economic sharing, and
the pursuit of justice. Ellul's generalization fits these
communities perfectly when he notes that "when communities with a 'style of life' of this kind have been
established, possibly the first signs of a new civilisation may begin to appear."[3]

Action
Engage in the subversive enterprise
of building Christian community.

The One City

*Clearly, large cities differ from each other. Yet
they have things in common. One of these is the
differentiation between poor neighborhoods and
those of the well-to-do.*

Rapid urbanization is a well-established feature of
the modern world. Over half of the world's population now live in large urban centers. While many
of the old myths about the city have been exploded,
some negative features remain constant. We have men-
tioned one such feature. Ellul identifies another. He
writes: "Venice, Paris, New York—they are all the same
city, only one Babylon always reappearing."[4]

And what characterizes "Babylon"? It is power,
wealth, trade, culture, and debauchery. This is the very
opposite of God's ideal, the New Jerusalem where there
is reconciliation and "the healing of the nations."
"Babylon" is the place of idolatry. It is the place where
the prophets are stoned. This is not to say that there
is nothing good in the modern city. It simply recognizes that the city celebrates mammon more than the
God of all the earth.

Reflection

*The city encapsulates the pride of
humans more than the glory of God.*

Fragile Victories

When God's quality of good emerges in our world, it will always be a surprise that is under threat from human control.

It is almost stating the obvious to acknowledge that there is good in our world. This is not in any way a denial of the presence of evil. Christians believe that this good is the fruit of God's grace bestowed on all people. Yet God always wishes to work a greater good in our world. This greater good is both personally redemptive and socially transformative. It is the drawing near of God's kingdom. It is the manifestation of the humanly impossible. It is when good things happen to not-so-good people. It occurs when social movements reflect kingdom values.

This is always a fragile but welcome victory. Ellul notes: "When peace timidly establishes itself, when justice reigns for a span, then it is fitting . . . that we should marvel and give thanks."[5] For when God's quality of good manifests itself in our world, it is a miracle in which we play a part, but which is wholly due to God's grace and power.

Reflection
*The good is always
God's miracle.*

The Language of Love

Love has its own reasons. Often love has no reasons at all.

Jacques Ellul believes that "the moment that a man and a woman love one another for something, whether it be for money or prestige or beauty or job, it's no longer love."[6] In other words, love is not essentially utilitarian. Love is motivated by the focus of its love. It seeks to serve and please the other for no other reason than that the other is the object of one's love. This is most mysterious and can hardly be comprehended, let alone explained.

All of this is not to suggest that love is not practical. But it is not just emotive. Love expresses itself in concrete good. But true love is self-forgetful. It not only focuses on the other; it also keeps no record of what it does. Love does not earn anything. It simply gives itself away.

Reflection

*Love finds its own ways to express and
to concretize itself. In doing this, it
seeks to benefit the other in ways
that affirm the other.*

Cry Justice

*A deep wound lies at the heart of the West. It is
its failure to practice justice.*

A strange irony characterizes the West. It was
responsible for articulating and enshrining in legislation the important matter of justice. Yet the
practice of justice has fallen far short of its ideals. Ellul
notes: "Western man claimed to be faithful to his wife,
but he multiplied his adulteries; egalitarian, but he
crushed the poor."[7]

The practice of justice is not only a pressing issue
in our law courts and the workplace. It is also an issue
in our homes and our churches. Women, for example,
often bear the "double burden." They are breadwin-
ners and homemakers. And in many churches, women
do the practical work of ministry, yet are denied appropriate status and position. At the heart of the New
Testament lies the radical message that the old barriers between ethnic, economic, and social groups
have been broken down. The challenge for us is therefore to practice this transformative message.

Action
*Do justice—it is closer to the heart of
God than our practice of worship.*

Doing It Anyway

*Never expect to win a popularity contest by
doing God's good in the world. Jesus showed us
that one may get crucified.*

There is a lot in contemporary Christianity that speaks
of blessing, success, well-being, power, and even
popularity. Some or all of these things may genuinely
come our way. But when they do, it is not because we
have worked out some amazing way to live the Christian
life. These things can only be the surprise of God's grace.

However, there is also another side to the
Christian life. This has to do with faithfulness in the
face of opposition, and perseverance in the midst of
difficulty and misunderstanding. Ellul makes the
point: "Do not expect others to appreciate you because
you are good and just."[8] In light of this reality, it may
be possible to set up a simple correlation. The more
we are seeking to do God's kind of good in our world,
the less popular we will be.

There is a simple reason for this. God's kind of
good has to do with the radical nature of God's kingdom. And that always involves repentance and change,
actions people often resent.

Action
*Be faithful in the face of opposition—it tests
the kind of stuff we are made of.*

New Possibilities

It is the insertion of new ideas, new initiatives, and new models that break the fossilization that pervades our world.

It is high time that we stopped being so naive about social reality! For even the good social structures and institutions that we create deteriorate. There are always diversionary impulses. The best legislation can be subtly subverted. And the most beneficent institutions can become self-serving. Thus the need to work for change is always with us. And change finds its genesis in hope.

Ellul reminds us that the "act of hope is . . . the opening up of situations which want to stay closed."[9] Hope always sees new possibilities. It sees what is not yet present, yet what ought to be. Hope never accepts present explanations and rationalizations. It does not accept the present impasse. It tenaciously refuses to accept that the present is all that there can be. Hope, instead, believes the future and embraces it.

Reflection
*Only in hope is the
new possible.*

Openings

To say that things may suddenly change for the better is not crass optimism. God is the One who opens up new opportunities.

L ife often has an almost monotonous regularity. But it also has its surprises. Cracks do appear in our seemingly concrete-like existence. The problem is not that no new opportunities occur, but that we have become mesmerized by our situation. We no longer see the openings in front of us or, if we do, we are no longer energized to take hold of the opportunity. Ellul reminds us that "we may not see any way out for now, but we should not claim that [no way out] exists."[10]

The problem with us is that we objectify our present reality and make it part of our inner world. Thus, we begin to think that this is the way things are; this is the way they are meant to be. As a result, we no longer believe that things can be different. The possibility that they can be is essential to our being human.

Reflection
If the Berlin Wall could suddenly come down, then change is always a possibility.

God's Benediction

There is little point in fervently praying God's blessing on what we want. We should seek to do what God wants. Then we may expect His blessing.

Ellul reminds us that "nothing remains of the work of man" if God does not give it effectiveness.[11] This is a sobering lesson. Much of what we do will simply pass away. It is of no value. Some of the things we do are downright harmful and negative. For these things we need to repent. But there are things we do that may have lasting value. These have to do with God's kingdom. They are things that are inspired by the Word of God. They are born out of prayer. They are activated by obedience. They are characterized by servanthood. They are motivated by love.

But even so, they require God's benediction and blessing. When we get everything right, we still need God's blessing. When the direction is clear, we still need God's anointing. When we have done all that we could do, God still needs to take things further. Our enough is never enough unless God's blessing rests upon it.

Reflection
*Much of what we do is in vain
unless we build with God's
direction and blessing.*

From Below

*We continue to believe that much needed change
will come from the power holders. Instead, we
should expect it to emerge from our committed
involvement with the poor and the marginalized.*

We look in the wrong place! We believe that
change will be top down, that those in power
will change the system to favor the needy. We are badly
mistaken! For those in power will finally favor the
powerful, in spite of all the rhetoric to the contrary.
Scraps of beneficence are thrown to the needy, but fundamental structural changes to benefit the poor
seldom occur.

Change, therefore, must come from below. Ellul
notes that "it is from the oppressed that there comes
the novelty that is needed if a society is to regain its
meaning and togetherness."[12] But this will only occur
when the poor or oppressed are infused with hope and
are mobilized to work for change. Here, the church can
be God's servant to the poor by joining them in their
struggle for change, freedom, and liberation.

Action
*Respond to the call to join the
oppressed for the sake of the gospel.
That is what working from below means.*

Why This Unhappiness?

One would expect that those who have made it to the top and enjoy wealth, power, and prestige would be happy. But they are not. Nor are those clamoring to get there.

Fundamentally, the human being is a sad creature. And many have advanced multiple reasons for this being so. The Christian perspective on this is most basic and yet most helpful. People are unhappy because they aspire to the good, but fail to achieve it. Being made in God's image, they have a vision of what is right. But because of their sinfulness, they are morally incapable of achieving their highest dreams and aspirations.

We rise, only to fall. We achieve, only to be disappointed. We work, only to remain unsatisfied. We love, only to remain unfulfilled. Ellul makes this observation about the modern person: "He is very busy, but he is emotionally empty."[13] This reflects the Christian position. We do not get what we think we deserve. Our labor, in the final analysis, does not satisfy.

Reflection
At an existential level, Christ lessens the pain of our present nonarrival at the final, ultimate experience by promising us fulfillment in the age to come.

Holiness

*The quest for holiness has nothing to do with
conformity to religious ritual. It is a purity
of the heart that motivates us to live boldly
in the world.*

One of the persistent scandals of Christianity is its
ability to inspire a spurious spirituality among its
adherents. Images, rituals, superstitions, and fears are
all part of this kaleidoscope of supposed virtue.
Underneath all this lies an unhealthy dualism, which
separates body and soul and church and world.
Adherence to these perspectives frequently emerges
out of a quest for certainty based on differentness. The
basic idea is: I am different from others, so I must be
pleasing to God.

Not only does this not follow, but it places
Christians in a highly defensive mode. As a result, we
are known for what we are against, not for what we
are and do. The issue here is our understanding of the
nature of holiness and sanctification. Ellul reminds us
that sanctification "does not mean making little angels
out of us, but setting us apart for the service that [God]
expects of us."[14]

Reflection
*Holiness sets us apart unto God in order that
we may make an impact on the world.*

Fruitfulness

*Fruitfulness comes from the grace and
enabling that God gives.*

A ctivism rather than passivity is the problem of the contemporary Christian. The pressing challenge, therefore, is not how to do more, but how to be more effective. Sometimes, effectiveness is related to doing less. This allows us to be more focused.

But effectiveness is also related to motivation and empowerment. Ellul reminds us that "when you have become weak and naked and powerless on account of your repentance, then you can begin to bring forth works that make sense and give life."[15] While fruit-fulness has to do with being properly trained and equipped, it also has to do with humility. Often our best efforts do not come from a position of strength, but from brokenness. It is in weakness that we are strong. It is in having nothing that we truly have some-thing to give. Sometimes, our skills can stand in the way of true effectiveness because we are relying on them rather than the power of God.

Reflection
*The Cross of Christ is the
power of weakness.*

The Cry of the Heart

*While I need to talk respectfully with God, I do
not need to talk carefully with Him. He can cope
with the cry of the heart.*

Prayer takes many forms. It can be a time of thanks-
giving or adoration. It can be a peaceful exchange.
But it can also be a stormy experience.

Ellul notes that "prayer is a striving with God."[16]
Is this a striving where we seek to coerce God? Or is
it a striving on behalf of others where our concern for
them becomes a "wrestling" with God? Or is our striving an earnest desire to know the will of God so that
we can live more authentically? Or is our striving a
search for blessings or answers that God does not seem
in a hurry to give?

Clearly, our striving will occur for many different reasons and with many differing motivations. But,
however good or bad those reasons may be, they are
far better than a sullen silence because we are in some
way disappointed in God.

Reflection
*Engagement is better
than withdrawal.*

Lord of All of Life

Jesus is not simply the Lord of my life and the church. His redemption embraces all reality.

Unlike many present-day Christians who only think about the implications of Jesus' victory for their own lives, the church of the Middle Ages grappled with understanding Christ's lordship of all life. For them, Ellul writes, "the God of Jesus Christ was the God of all reality: everything belonged to him, including the economic and social orders."[17]

While we can debate how well the church of that time understood its task and, more particularly, actually performed, they were at least asking the right questions. It is high time that we should begin to grapple with similar questions. We need to break away from our narrow spirituality and our churchly preoccupations. For after all, the church is not really an end in itself. It is a servant of the kingdom of God. And because that kingdom is all-embracing, Christians should also engage in nation building. The institutions of our land also need God's transforming grace.

Action
*While you are in the marketplace,
just as much as in the churches,
be God's change agents.*

Witness of the Spirit

*A world devoid of the Spirit becomes a world
dominated by technique. A world with the Spirit
is a world open to renewal and truth.*

There is nothing so barren as a world devoid of
dreams. Hope. Creativity. Surprise. The in-breaking
of the Spirit. There is nothing so rigid as institutions run
as bureaucracies. Without humanity. Without flexibility. Without openness to the winds of change. And there
is nothing so pitiful as a church with dogma, liturgy, and
projects, but without inspiration, joy, and grace.

If there is to be any hope and renewal, then the
breath of the Spirit must be present. If any empowerment is to occur, then the incubating presence of the
Spirit must be there. If true community is to be
achieved rather than the pseudo-community of pleas-
antries and superficialities, then the galvanizing and
unifying work of the Spirit must be operative. And as
Ellul rightly points out: "If people are to recognise the
truth, they must also have the inner witness of the Holy
Spirit."[18]

Reflection

*Without the Spirit, we are locked into the
prisons of our own creations. With the Spirit,
we are free to start again and to fly.*

People Empowerment

One of the great challenges of our time is for people to come out from under the sway of guardians and experts in order that they may take greater responsibility for their own lives.

Not only is it true, as Ellul states, that in our modern society "the state gradually assumes responsibility for all the activities of society,"[19] but we are increasingly becoming expert-led and expert-dependent. Every aspect of our lives has come under careful scrutiny and for every problem we have someone to provide a professional assessment and a hoped-for cure. Instead of all this wonderful knowledge freeing us, it has made us anxious and less than self-reliant. Common sense has departed from our lives as we rely more and more on others to give us information and to guide our lives. Even the church, the household of faith, functions as an institution led by religious experts.

The time has come for us to reclaim our heritage. In Christ we are brothers and sisters, not backward children. Therefore, we need to take responsibility for how we are church and how we share life together.

Reflection
*Taking responsibility is
the key to maturity.*

Taking the Risk

While new ways of being and doing need to
emerge in faith and hope, they cannot proceed
without taking risks.

It is more than reasonable to calculate carefully the possible outcomes of some new project. To weigh options. To deliberate on future possibilities. To think about possible consequences. To anticipate possible hindrances and blockages. It is also more than reasonable to plan and pray. Discuss and discern. Consult and listen to your inner self. Believe and calculate. Hope and evaluate.

But after all this, one can only proceed by being willing to take risks. An unwillingness to take this step leaves one in the realm of the probable, not in the pursuit of the possible. Jacques Ellul rightfully reminds us that "the more security and guarantees we want against things, the less free we are."[20] And in the pursuit of the new, no guarantees are possible except the risk of faith and the participation of the God of surprises.

Action
Make the move to proceed and so
put yourself wholly in God's hands.

To Will and to Do

*No matter how much we are tempted to
withdraw from the world because we think
that we will not make much of a difference,
we are called to will and to do.*

In one sense we are hopelessly caught. We know that
in spite of Christ's wonderful victory, the fallenness,
pain, violence, and folly of this world continue. In the
two thousand years of the church's long history, it has
never seen complete victory. On the other hand, both
Jesus and the Spirit continue to challenge us to work
and pray for a better world and the coming of God's
final kingdom.

Hence, we are caught between bitter realism and
the glance of faith. If we do not act, nothing changes.
Ellul is clear about this: "If we do not pray, if we do
not do the works of faith, if we do not seek after wisdom, if we do not preach the gospel, nothing in history
nor . . . in the church would look much different."[21]
However, if we do all these things, there is no guarantee of final victory either. There is only the blessing
of faithfulness.

Reflection
*Having done all, we are only
unprofitable servants.*

Hope and the Kingdom

*The loss of an ability to try again is often
due to a loss of hope.*

While the kingdom of God will not be fully realized in this age because we continue to
experience the fallenness of our world, we are to pray
and work that more and more of God's kingdom will
come amongst us. The vision of kingdom is born out
of hope. And hope empowers us for action.

Ellul reminds us that "if hope does not rivet us
to . . . action, then the kingdom of God within us
becomes a meaningless, sterile contemplation."[22] In
other words, hope is never enough. It can become mere
daydreaming. Hope needs to be the galvanizer. It draws
us forward. It mesmerizes us to attempt to realize our
dreams. Thus, hope leads to risk-taking and action.
Hope provides both the shape of our godly expectations and the drive to make them happen.

Action
*Act out of hope and so seek
to bring in the new.*

Revolutionary Change

Christians have a role, not so much to preserve the world, but to change it.

The language of revolution, let alone the action of revolution, sits most uncomfortably with many Christians. They have the idea that the Christian task in the world is one of peacemaking and healing only. This is one-sided, for it may mean merely preserving the status quo. Christians also have the task of bringing about change and transformation. Ellul points out that "in order to preserve the world, it is actually necessary that a genuine revolution should take place."[23]

There are many forms of revolution, such as political, industrial, and cultural. We can speak also of the need for a spiritual revolution that has both personal and societal implications. This means that personal transformation through Christ leads to a changed lifestyle, a radical form of being the people of God and seeing the kingdom come to expression in all areas of life.

Reflection
*If the church does not demonstrate
a radical lifestyle, it can hardly
seek to change the world.*

Challenge

*Jesus brings both blessing and challenge
to our lives.*

Jacques Ellul reminds us that "the one who suffered,
who was crucified and raised in his glorified body, still
speaks to me today with words that burn, that start me
off and push me into being something other than what
I am."[24] Jesus is not a mere figure of the past. His is a
living present. Through His Word and Spirit, He continues to address me at the very center of my being. He
brings to me not only words of affirmation and encouragement, but also the challenge of transformation.

Jesus never leaves me where I am. That would be
a tragedy! I need to move forward even though I am
reluctant. I need cleansing even when I think that there
is nothing wrong with me. I need renewal even when
I think that I am spiritually strong. I need grace to take
me further in God's purpose for my life.

Reflection
*Christ's transforming work
is both firm and gentle.*

Work and Generosity

Work is intrinsic to our spirituality. It is not just a part of our normal life; it is part of our life lived before God.

God is a worker. He is the God who created and maintains. We are also workers. But we are called to work in partnership with God, fulfilling His will and expressing His kingdom values in every sphere of life.

Ordinary work is not outside of God's purpose. Both the marketplace and the monastery are places where we can serve God. The one is not inferior to the other. The mechanic and the preacher both have a duty to serve God in their respective spheres of work.

The purpose of work is manifold. We are to serve those for whom we work. But we are also to serve those who benefit from our work. Ellul states simply: "God gives you work so that you can have something to give in turn."[25] In all of this is a simple cycle: We receive in order that we may give.

Action
Allow work to issue in generosity so that the power of work is broken in your life.

Western Values

There is much that the West can celebrate. Its technological and artistic achievements are awesome. But the West is hardly placed to be the moral guardian of the world. Its own house is not in order.

While the West continues to flaunt its technological prowess, its moral and spiritual impact on life is like a fading star. Christian leadership is shifting to the Third World. And the vitality of Christianity will come more and more from that part of the world rather than from the West. Ellul points out that the West has been such a bundle of extremes. "Greatness and shame, utilitarianism and charity, generosity and exploitation" all jostle together in the history that is uniquely the West's.[26]

Yet no matter how bad things may be, the possibility of transformation is always with us. While history lasts, there is no final estimation. Renewal is always a possibility. The church can play a critical role in the renewal of the West. But the church will first need to become much surer of its own faith and achieve the moral will to work passionately for change.

Action
Work to create a church that is a transformed community so that it can be a transforming influence in the world.

Life in the Spirit

It is not so much a matter of us possessing the Spirit. It is much more a matter of the Spirit possessing us.

God is sovereign. He also draws near to us. But in drawing close through the Spirit, God does not come under our control. God is always free in His purposes. Ellul therefore gives us an important warning. "We talk of having faith, of having the Holy Spirit, not of living in and by faith, of receiving and being sent forth by the Holy Spirit."[27]

We need this reminder. The Spirit beautifies our life with the fruit of patience, love, and self-control, but this is to make us more like Christ. The Spirit empowers us, but this is so that we can serve the purposes of God's kingdom better. The Spirit imparts wisdom, but this is so that we can live a life of greater faithfulness. Moreover, the Spirit leads us; we don't direct the Spirit.

Action
*Be obedient, for that is the
key to the Spirit-filled life.*

Building Community

*The task of the church is to build family, the
church community, and neighborliness. The
church also has a role in nation building.*

Ellul reminds us that "Christianity claims to be sub-
stituting love for order, fraternity for hierarchy,
freedom for law."[28] That it hasn't always achieved this
should be self-evident. But whenever Christianity has
been faithful to the roots from which it sprang, these
characteristics are present.

And the key to these features is the practice of
building community. This involves the practice of
openness. Sharing our common stories. Building
bridges of trust. Sharing mutual burdens and concerns.
Practical help. Encouraging each other in the faith.
Celebrating important events in our lives. Breaking
bread. The practice of common prayers. The mutual
listening to Scripture. From building Christian community together, we learn skills and gain inspiration
to practice this in our families, neighborhoods, and
places of employment.

Action
*Work for community. The church can
have any and every form or structure,
but it must provide community.*

Hospitality

While we are greatly pressured to pull up the drawbridge when it comes to our own home life, the challenge is to lower it for the practice of hospitality.

Ellul writes: "An inseparable couple, a united couple, is an extraordinary force on behalf of the lonely, the suffering, the deprived."[29] He is not speaking theoretically at this point. This he practiced even though he was a busy academic, a prolific writer, and an active churchperson. And this ministry of hospitality he could only achieve in genuine partnership with his wife. Together, they would have decided to live this way and, together, they would have carried the burdens and joys of this kind of lifestyle.

Having known something of the reality of this in my own life, I challenge the reader to do the same. This has nothing to do with turning your home into a hostel. It simply means that we incorporate into our lives and homes the ones and twos that God sends our way.

Action
Make room for the needy; it is often a blessing for the giver.

Beyond Blessings

*Faithfulness to God must always be a
commitment beyond the blessings He gives.*

Ellul is adamant: "I remain faithful to God, even if
nothing, absolutely nothing more comes my way
from him."[30] This is a powerful confession. It looks
beyond gifts to the giver. It looks beyond blessings to
the source of life. It is an acknowledgment that in
knowing God I need nothing more.

In knowing the God who has redeemed me in
Jesus Christ, I need nothing else. I already have the gift
of eternal life. My eyes have been opened. My heart is
changed. Fellowship with God is restored. I am part of
the new humanity in Christ. I have received the gift of
the Spirit. What more do I want? What more do I need?
The reality is that I need nothing else. But God so often
pours out those extra surprises that make life full.

Reflection

*It is almost as if God can't help Himself. He
gives so much more than what we need.*

OCTOBER

Disruption

*God does not come merely to affirm what is
good in the world; He also comes to call things
into question and to effect change.*

God's commitment to change the world involves
changing the church. It is only a changed church
that can effect change in the world. God therefore
comes to disturb our solemn assemblies. Ellul points
out that "the church institution can be valid only if
there is interference, shock, overturning, and initiative on the part of God . . . [otherwise] it is a purely
sociological body."[1] The church so readily devolves into
an institution that provides religious goods and services and champions the cause of the status quo.

The church, however, should be something quite
different. It is called to be a community of people who
live to the sound of a different drum. They are a people
who live kingdom values and are the change agents in
society. They are people characterized by God's disturbing presence in their lives.

Reflection
*Disruption is a blessing if it
leads to transformation.*

A Sacred Responsibility

Christians do not have an advantage over other people. Their commitment merely puts them in a position to serve other people.

Some Christians are doggedly triumphalistic. They believe that they will experience better health and greater wealth because God is on their side. Some Christians even believe that they are best placed to rule society. God has given them, they claim, greater gifts and wisdom than those who are outside of Christ.

This is elitist thinking. It has little to do with reality. Being a Christian does not make one a special person in the social sense. Being a Christian confers no such special privileges. Ellul rightly points out that "being a Christian is neither a privilege, nor an advantage, but a charge and a mission."[2] We cannot use the blessings and gifts of God for our own advantage. We cannot use the power of the Spirit to become powerful people. If we do this, that very power will destroy us.

Reflection
We are saved to serve. We are empowered to serve. And we are blessed to serve.

The Will to Power

Power is part of human existence. It cannot be wished away by the priority of love. But the exercise of power can be conditioned by love so that it becomes true servanthood.

Ellul is characteristically blunt: "The spirit of power lies deep in the human heart."[3] This in no way means that we all aspire to become dictators. It may simply mean that we want to be in control of our own existence and be able to influence others. Nor does it necessarily mean that we all want to be overt leaders. We may simply wish to stimulate people through our art or music or influence them through our writing.

Yet in all of this we do exercise power. Whether we exercise the power of force or the power of gentle persuasion, we are exercising power. The critical issue is not that we seek to use power. It is that we utilize power for beneficial ends. Rather than power for self, we are called to use power for the benefit of others.

Reflection
We need to guard particularly against working under the guise of helping others when in fact we are merely benefiting ourselves.

Attentiveness

*It is always more important that we listen to
God than that He listens to us.*

Prayer is the art of dialogue. It is the art of two
people speaking and responding. The one should
not dominate the other. It must never be a one-way
process. It should be interactive. Having cried to God,
having spoken what is on my heart or mind, I become
a candidate for careful listening. Jacques Ellul reminds
us that "the true relation in prayer is not when God
hears what is prayed for, but when the person praying continues to pray until he is the one who hears,
who hears what God wills."[4]

This in no way undermines the value of our
speaking to God. It highlights instead that in our
speaking to God, God desires to gain our attention. In
praying we are also to listen. For God desires to speak
to us as much as He is willing to help us. While His
help may focus on the immediate, His speaking to us
may give us life direction.

Reflection
*Getting beyond speaking to the place of
solitude puts us in a position to hear.*

The Devil's Work

The worst form of evil comes under the guise of the appearance of good.

The secret of the Christian life is to have the power to do what is good and the discernment to know what is evil. When evil is very evil, the Devil usually has overplayed his hand. When evil masquerades as good, we know that Satan is working most effectively. Ellul notes: "Typical of the way the devil acts [is] pretending to accomplish God's work while transforming it into its opposite."[5]

Unfortunately, we often come to this realization when it is much too late. Usually it takes years, sometimes decades, to see clearly the end result of our grandiose schemes. And it is even more difficult for us to admit that we have been building on sand and, worse, playing into the hands of the Enemy. Yet we need to learn to avoid these mistakes and therefore need to encourage in our communities the use of the gift of discernment. We need people who are prepared to ask the hard and critical questions rather than creating an atmosphere of acquiescence.

Action
Be suspicious and questioning.
Your community needs such a gift.

Means

*The modern idea that if something works well it
must be right has filtered into the very fabric of
the church.*

The old ethical debate between means and ends has
almost become passé. The idea that the end does
not necessarily justify the means is hardly believed any-
more. Sadly, the more prevalent idea is that, as long
as there are "successful" outcomes, the methods used
to achieve these should not be scrutinized.

There is also a flip side to this attitude: There can
be such a focus on means that the end result is lost
from view. Ellul is particularly concerned about this
approach. He points out that we are to fight "against
our present enslavement to means."[6] This magnifies
technique, methods, procedures, management, and
processes. It fails, however, to see the larger picture.
Our ecological plunder is a good example of the mag-
nification of means and a loss of end results. In the
church also we have overemphasized management
techniques and have failed to see how this destroys the
church as community.

Reflection
*One cannot build the
church as community if one does
not use community-building processes.*

The Manageable God?

Instead of a God who blazes at injustice, we have created the docile God who lovingly forgives and forgets the inhumanity of our world.

The church's princes, the theologians, have often been less than helpful in their formulations regarding the nature and character of God. Some have made God so wholly other that He is unreachable. Some have made Him so futuristic that He is inaccessible. Some have made God so immanent that He cannot be distinguished from the world. Some have made Him so loving that He has become condoning. But some have virtually emasculated God.

Ellul fulminates that the God of the prophets has now become "a senile Good Shepherd whose beard all the world might tug."[7] One of the reasons why we have produced the docile God is because we foolishly think that God has failed to enter the modern arena to save us from our own folly. Little do we realize that He has entered the fray, but has left us to taste the fruits of our own machinations.

Reflection

God is no more manageable than an artist's inspiration, a lover's dream, a prophet's passion, and a visionary's articulation of a new world.

Nonconformity

The church can only be a counter-community.
If it is anything other than that, it has already
compromised itself.

Except for those who live only for heaven and have
never responded to the cry of the earth, most
Christians rightly believe that they have a task here. How
this task is understood varies with different Christians.
Some see the task as only evangelistic. Others see it as
comprehensively as nation building. The threat facing
the church in all of this, however, is that it uses
worldly means to achieve spiritual ends. Moreover, the
church throughout its long history has generally failed
to handle power and influence successfully.

Ellul's reminder is apposite when he states that "our
only guarantee of efficacy is the achievement of nonconformity."[8] What he means is that the success of the
church can only lie in its being a counter-community.
It is when the church conforms more to the kingdom
of God than to worldly strategies that it will be a powerful force in the world.

Reflection
If the church is not different from the world,
it cannot offer the world anything.

Strength for the Journey

To be rescued is a helpful but not necessarily an empowering process. To become strong means learning to go through difficulty.

A lot of praying presupposes the desire to be rescued. We want God to bring us relief. We want to be snatched out of our difficult circumstances. Sometimes this is most appropriate.

But this is not the way we can live the whole of our lives. Rather than being rescued, we also need to learn to persevere in tough times. When God empowers us instead of rescuing us, this does not mean that He has failed to answer our prayers. It simply means that He is answering our prayers in a way that is different from what we expected.

Ellul rightly points out that "your prayer is answered, not because the situation is miraculously cleared up, but because you have been granted exactly as much strength and ability . . . as is necessary."[9] To be provided with strength for the journey, particularly walking the rough road, is as much a sign of God's grace as it is to be rescued out of all our troubles.

Reflection
*God is committed to
journeying with us.*

Work

While work is an ideal place for building community, it is so often the place of conflict and strife.

Work is most often difficult. It can be difficult through its complexity, but also through its meaninglessness. But the difficulty of work is compounded by relationship issues. Work by its very nature requires cooperation and partnership. It is premised on the notion of community. The workplace should be the place of people in solidarity.

But Ellul reminds us that "work corrupts human relationships. Instead of solidarity through work, [we find] domination and hostility."[10] The workplace is frequently a place of conflict. It is not simply conflict between management and workers. There is also ideological conflict, reflecting different perspectives about how to achieve common objectives. Yet it is precisely this kind of workplace that needs the redemptive presence of Christ. It is precisely in this kind of environment that Christians should pursue peace on the basis of justice and where they should demonstrate the servant qualities of their Master.

Action
In the workplace, work to achieve the common good. We are not there simply to further our own careers.

Suspicion

Christians can never afford to be gullible. Their
faith empowers them to face the real world.

Christians live in hope. One of their major hopes is
that, at the end of history, God will establish a new
world. But Christians also have hopes for this world.
The most basic is that this world will become a better
place through the breaking in of God's kingdom.

These hopes, based on Scripture, can never
become a Utopian or political dream. And the way to
achieve these hopes has little to do with economic programs. Therefore, Christians need to be discerning that
they do not confuse worldly agendas with the reality
of God's reign. Ellul reminds us that "we have to find
behind the theories which . . . blind us from every
quarter, the reality which they hide from us."[11] In other
words, we have to exercise suspicion. Many programs
look good, but in the end are still elitist and self-
serving. Christian good is always redemptive and
other-serving. This puts them out of step with the
world's agenda.

Reflection
We need to reflect carefully on the means
we use to achieve certain goals.

Powerlessness

*While we cannot radically change our world,
we can live our lives trying.*

Ellul rightly reminds us that we must face the "experience of the powerlessness of each of us in [the] face of the world."[12] Even though we have by faith experienced Christ's redemptive power, we are still so limited in what we can do. We ourselves are hardly fully changed. Old patterns of thinking and doing persist. Old fears remain. Old insecurities continue to threaten us in our forward movement.

Our churches are also places where change is difficult. We constantly need to pray and work for God's kingdom to break into our ecclesiastical traditions and priorities. And when it comes to affecting our neighborhoods and our world, we are only too aware of our weaknesses and limitations.

This note of utter realism is not a recipe for inactivity. It simply guards against Utopianism. In working for change against such great odds, we are simply acknowledging that God can bless both our small and great efforts.

Action
*The small is not always significant,
but start on the small as a way to
begin doing the significant.*

Weaving a Mosaic

*In the daily rhythm of a life of faith and
responsibility, we weave a pattern of existence
that is the miracle of God's grace incarnated in
ordinary affairs.*

While it is true that so much has already been
given to us by virtue of our biology and
upbringing, it is also true that we are intimately
involved in shaping our lives. In particular, we have
a hand in finetuning the moral quality of our lives.
Ellul points out that "our lives are made up of
works—not only great works, but daily activities, relations with family and associates, words that we speak,
decisions that we make in politics or love."[13]

None of this, no matter how small, is lost. While
it may not have radically impacted on our world, it is
not lost to God, who accepts even our smallest gifts.
Nor is it lost on ourselves. For in the daily rhythm of
life, we are subtly shaping our very being and creating an environment for those who are in our immediate
sphere of influence—family and friends.

Reflection
*It is what we are in the intimacy of family
and friends that should also characterize
us in our social and professional life.*

Change

*Meaningful change is both born out of hope
and is sustained by hope.*

The reality of ongoing change is a fact of life. We age and things decay. The need to effect change in our social and institutional realities is real. The systems we create soon become outmoded and stultify. Change, therefore, should be welcomed rather than ardently resisted, because it is change that brings about new possibilities. And this can only spring from hope. As Ellul points out: "Hope is the creator of history, since it opens the closed, hardened and self-contained situations."[14]

But our hopes need to be grounded in more than mere optimism or idealism. Many a hope has been dashed on those rocks that lie ever so threateningly below a calm expanse of water. Hope needs the certainty that God is leading the way and is calling us to faithfulness and commitment. And God's Word needs to shape the broad contours of our hope so that it conforms to the kingdom of God's grace and justice.

Action
*As change agents, learn to laugh at present
certainties and call them into question.*

An Impersonal World

*In the midst of our technological world we may
well be losing something of our humanity.*

Modern technology has given us so much. We not
only have the means to further control and exploit
nature, but we also have found ways to control and
manipulate our inner psyche.

Yet this has been a mixed blessing. We are awed
by what we can make. We are pleased with what med-
ical technology can do for us. We make use of the
psychological technologies to help us cope. But we also
increasingly feel rootless and alienated in the world we
are creating.

Ellul reminds us that "we have no choice but to
live in this technological world; but we are forced to
find something providing satisfaction elsewhere."[15]
Because technology so readily overwhelms the individual, we need to find ways to reassert our humanity
and individuality. We need to build community in our
cities of anonymity and partnership and participation
in our bureaucracies.

Action
*Ensure that our technologies
do not become idolatrous.*

Victory

There is constantly the possibility of significant change in the present. But this only occurs when God gives us the victory.

Our lives are not locked into ironclad certainties or historical necessity. While there are powerful socializing forces, we can make choices and live to the sound of a different drummer. And while we remain in a fallen world, we do experience the love and grace of God. This grace not only frees us from sin's deadly power, but it also empowers us to do battle against all that is evil in our world.

Ellul remarks that "because the demons are stripped of their power in eternity, we too can win the victory in time."[16] To win such victories, we will need to deal not only with the personal effects of evil, but also with institutional evil. The greatest way in which the Devil can attack us is when we accept unjust structures as normal. In that way, we are beaten even before we do battle.

Reflection

The Holy Spirit empowers us not only to break the powers of bondage, but also to discern what is good and evil in our world.

Commitment

The Christian life is not one commitment,
but a lifetime of commitments.

It is true that God is faithful in His commitment to us. He will not allow us to be snatched out of His hand. It is equally true that we need to be faithful in our commitment to God. And in one sense, that commitment needs to be made again and again. For every day we are faced with small decisions, each of which can be a starting point for going in the wrong direction.

Ellul states rather strongly that "whether for power or for happiness, man is always ready to leave his Lord."[17] The temptation to unfaithfulness is always with us. And often it is an accumulation of many small decisions that finds us in deep trouble. But it is the experience of such trouble that holds hope for us. For it is precisely at that point that we can come to our senses and cry out to God for mercy, help, and grace.

Reflection

It is far better to make many small steps of
faithfulness than to place our hope in being
rescued inches from the brink.

Freedom

The desire for freedom continues to flicker in the human heart, nourished by the oil of God.

Gaining an adequate understanding of what freedom is will always elude us. We are better at sensing when we are not free, even though we are not sure how to move forward. The way forward can only come by way of illumination or inspiration.

But "once the possibility of freedom is glimpsed, nothing else can satisfy man."[18] Ellul is right, for there is nothing that can so motivate and mobilize people as a vision of new possibilities based upon the sense that present realities are intolerable and only the new is just. Such a vision will inspire people to give their best, to give their all.

Sadly for some, such a vision never comes. They never question what is and therefore never ask anything new of the future. For others, such a vision does come. When it does, grab it with both hands. You may only get one chance.

Reflection

If we don't seize the day, we will only inherit the night.

Silence

*There is a legitimate silence where we keep to
ourselves the privacy of our innermost thoughts.
But silence should never be used as a weapon
against other people.*

Ellul laments his relationship with someone: "He
falls silent, and I no longer know where or how
to take my place in relation to him."[19] Here, silence has
become a barrier. It may even be the weapon that renders the other person as nonperson. Silence so often
means that I have already made a decision and ren-
dered a judgment. I have nothing more to say. I have
made up my mind.

Yet the possibility for reconciliation is premised
on talking together. The possibility of gaining further
insight or coming to a different position is premised on
communication. Therefore, I cannot afford to fall into
silence, for silence provides no possibility for forward
movement.

Reflection
*While there does come a time when a particu-
lar issue can be no longer discussed profitably,
building and maintaining relationships does
require ongoing communication.*

Never Enough

*When we have done all to bring about personal,
institutional, and social change, we still have
not achieved God's goal.*

To know that we cannot achieve all that God asks
of us in our task of being salt and light in the world
is not an argument for passivity. The opposite is the
case. It is an argument for prayerful and faithful work,
but against thinking that we can bring in the kingdom
of God.

Jacques Ellul reminds us that one error is the idea
that "by achieving certain reforms we shall have
reached the order that God wills."[20] The best conversions require further growth. The most "successful"
churches require the fresh wind of the Spirit. Our best
efforts at community development can eventually fall
into disrepair and the most spectacular revival can
burn itself out within a generation. Therefore, the task
continues both in times of difficulty and success, even
more so in times of success.

Reflection
*Success can be the great enemy of
further necessary progress.*

Discernment

*While Christians should be, above all, full of
faith and hope, they should not be naive and
gullible.*

Whether we like it or not, we are in a spiritual battle. The forces of the fallen world and the
impulses of the Spirit of God are in conflict. In such
circumstances, Christians need to be discerning so that
they don't call good evil and evil good. The task of discernment is never easy, for we sometimes cannot get
clear guidelines from Scripture. There are many ethical issues that the Bible does not directly address.

Hence, we have the difficult task of applying broad
biblical principles to specific contemporary issues. But
it is not only a matter of understanding the Bible. It is
also a matter of understanding our world. We need to
discern what are the forces for good and evil in our era.
In all of this, Ellul reminds us that "the discernment
of spirits can be accomplished only through prayer."[21]

Action

*Be prayerful in understanding Scripture,
our world, and particularly our value
judgments and presuppositions.*

Facing Challenges

*We don't have to look for challenges. They will
come our way. The critical issue is whether we
will face them or flee.*

There is nothing static about life. It is constantly
evolving. But things do not automatically develop
for the better. Things can also deteriorate. As a result
of this to and fro movement, we are always faced with
challenges. Ellul comments that "every society, like
every individual, faces challenges and will evolve
according to its ability to take them up, to absorb them,
or to neutralize them."[22]

To flee is simply to abandon our responsibility
and to accept the status quo. To face life's challenges
is to embrace the risk of growth. But facing challenges
requires more than courage. It also requires wisdom
and discernment. Some challenges will lead us into
side alleys. Others will creatively carry us forward. We
need God's help to know which is which.

Reflection
*Growth always involves some pain
and responding to life's challenges
is one way of painful growth.*

The Big Questions

*Many of life's big questions revolve around what
can I know, how should I live, and what may
I hope for?*

It is rather obvious that faith has as much to do with
the meaning of life in this world as with the fulfillment of life in the world to come. If faith only has
relevance for the future life, it renders the present as
unimportant. This will result in a world-denying
form of Christianity. If, on the other hand, faith is only
relevant for the present, it denies the power of future
hope. This will result in a worldly Christianity that
confuses present realities with the kingdom of God.

Yet the power of faith is to make the present
meaningful and livable. If this is to occur, faith must
assist us, writes Ellul, to know "where we come from,
where we are going, how we are situated, what our
future is."[23] Faith in the light of God's revelation in
Christ can help us with these questions and also to
understand our present situation. We can see that this
fallen world is marked by God's grace and that God
has promised to journey with us in all of our life's
circumstances.

Reflection
*To life's big questions, there are only
unfolding rather than final answers.*

Hope Has a Future

*Hope is not simply the impulse without which
life would be meaningless. It is also the gateway
that beckons the future.*

There almost seems to be an ironclad certainty about
the technological development of the modern world.
History seems to have its predictable laws of progress.
With fate banished from the modern mind, only scientific certainties remain.

But for the Christian, nothing is inevitable. Because
God, rather than economics, rules the world, there are
always new possibilities. God continues to interrupt the
smooth flow of history. He joins the poor in their struggle and brings down the mighty who proudly exult in
their power and exploit the powerless. Because God is
always ahead of us, our calling is not passively to resign
ourselves to the inevitable, but to anticipate in hope
God's involvement in our lives and in our world. Hence,
we work for change. We pray for a fuller manifestation
of God's kingdom. We live in the hope that the God who
is ahead of us will bless us with His future.

Reflection
*Without hope, only the present remains.
In hope, the future joins us. In the
words of Ellul: "Hope . . . forces
the future to show its hand."*[24]

Risk Taking

Faith does not look at certainties, but at possibilities.

While we may long for the smooth flow of continuity and tradition, life that is meaningful involves transition, change, and renewal. And to invite change and renewal involves faith and risk taking. Ellul reminds us that "if you start taking everything into account, you will do nothing and arrive nowhere."[25]

Life is not premised on absolute certainties. Instead, it is based on the power of faith. While faith appreciates the past and celebrates the present, it always looks for new possibilities. And exploring new possibilities always involves risk taking. Such risk taking involves flexibility and an open-ended approach to life. It also involves courage to attempt the new. But above all, it involves prayer.

The person of faith, in prayer, moves forward, knowing that God has opened the future.

Reflection

To attempt the new is always in the category of faith rather than in the province of certainty.

Generalizations

*The more we generalize, the more we reduce our
existence to comfortable mediocrity.*

While the Gospel writers may well have attempted
to systematize the sayings and actions of Jesus,
they failed to achieve this by the sheer nature of the
material they had to work with. Jesus' words did not
lend themselves to building theological systems and
His actions were anything but predictable. Jesus'
words were like flashes of light and inspiration. His
deeds were clear statements of authenticity and
integrity.

Jesus, therefore, was much more like a social revolutionary than an academic. He sought to bring about
social transformation by both rich and poor living the
lifestyle of the kingdom of God, a kingdom based on
reconciliation, love, mercy, and justice. To generalize
about the words of Jesus is to depower them. They
need to be heard in the depths of the heart and reck-
lessly lived in the power of faith.

Reflection
*Ellul writes: "Generalisations
destroy meaning."*[26]

A Beam of Light

*The Word of God can strike home and challenge
us to the very core of our being.*

Like everything else, Scripture can also become
familiar and powerless. In fact, the Bible can fall
silent. And when it does, life takes on a prosaic character. This is not to suggest that life should always be
full of changes and surprises. Life must also have its
legitimate routines. But life needs its creative moments.

Jacques Ellul, in speaking of the Bible, says that
"suddenly a phrase becomes a personal utterance. It
penetrates into your life."[27] This occurs when the Word
of God empowered by the Holy Spirit breaks in like a
shaft of light and impels our life in a new direction.

For some, such a word has been the call to work
with the poor and disenfranchised of the earth. For others, such a word has resulted in a life of meditation and
prayer. While discernment is required when a word
strikes home, we can be much surer that it is from God
when such a word has to do with serving God's kingdom rather than simply benefiting ourselves.

Reflection
*A word from God can truly
revolutionize one's life.*

Faith

Faith is strong enough to face the world, no matter how difficult life's circumstances may be.

Faith is not a flight from reality. It is the opposite. Faith is a trust in God, who journeys with us in all of life's situations. Faith does not negate life. It affirms it. Faith does not escape the world. It builds it. For faith has a vision of the kingdom of God and sees what God's new world can be like in the midst of the broken structures of our own making.

As Ellul rightly points out, we need to reject "belief as a refuge and flight from reality, the degradation of faith when it is seized upon as protection, as a guarantee or insurance policy."[28] Faith is none of these things. It certainly can't manipulate God and it is no protection from the rigors and challenges of life. Faith instead looks to God when we are most inclined to trust in our own ability.

Reflection

Faith doesn't always ask God to do things for us. Faith also asks God to strengthen us for the task He has set for us.

Human Ingenuity

While human creativity should be encouraged at all times, in the matter of faith we are called to submit to God's revelation.

Human creativity is a wonderful gift from God. With it we are to fulfill God's mandate to shape and care for our world. And with this gift we are to make things beautiful as well as orderly. But our giftedness is to find its center in the will of God. Creativity is not without boundaries and it doesn't exist for itself. Human creativity is to find its pinnacle in the service of God. Left by itself, it can easily become self-serving.

Nowhere is this more evident than in the area of religion. Ellul points out that "if man is left to his own resources and acts according to his own design, he will necessarily reconstruct a religion."[29] Here, creativity goes astray. Here, creativity serves the creature rather than the God who has so abundantly imparted His gifts to us.

Reflection
All men and women, including artists, can serve the kingdom.

Nonconformity

*While it is legitimate to play a maintenance
role, we also need the creative change agents.*

Human life is profoundly social. And everywhere we have created institutions that serve us.
The church is one such institution among many others, including schools, hospitals, and many other
welfare services. Much effort is required to maintain
such institutions.

Yet they also need to respond to change in order
to become more effective. While many institutions
demand loyalty and conformity, they need the impulse
of the nonconformists. Ellul reminds us that "an institution does not survive on its own. It can exist only
by way of either violence or the ritualisation that guarantees conformity without judgment."[30] If institutions
are to remain healthy, they need to respond to creative
change. And this will require the courage of those who
use their creative judgment.

Action
*Work for change, even though it is always
a risky undertaking. Such work takes not
only wisdom, but also courage. But
taking these risks shows a greater loyalty
than maintaining the status quo.*

Change

*If we simply affirm the realities of our world
without also seeking to change them, then we
are not the salt and light that God calls us to be.*

Ours is a beautiful world and there is so much among us that is good and true. But there is also much that is both tragic and demonic. Ours is a world marred by sin and characterized by injustice. But even so, there are signs everywhere of the presence of the kingdom of God, there are the pockets of hope, there are the sons and daughters of the kingdom who in the power of the Spirit are God's instruments for change.

Ellul simply states: "We believe that God's promise, received in faith, borne by us, truly changes the conditions in which we live."[31] God is actively caring for His world and we need to join Him in faith and trust to fulfill His purposes.

Action

*God has neither abandoned nor is inactive
in our world. Join His program to
bring about significant change.*

NOVEMBER

Complementarity

*While so much of life is characterized by
superior and inferior relations, the impulse of
holism is complementarity.*

Even though so much of life abounds with hierarchies and distinctions, the genius of life is holism.
Soul and body are vitally interconnected. A clear conscience, for example, has implications for good health.

Similarly in other areas of life, it is partnership
that will lead us forward, rather than the chronic idea
that we can go it alone and that we don't really need
anyone else. Jacques Ellul reminds us that "complementarity is not in sexuality alone, but in the totality
of life."[1] Women and men together need to build a
better world. Leaders and those being led need to find
new ways to join hands in common endeavors.
Helpers and those being helped need to discover
strategies for cooperation.

Action
*If we hope and dream alone, we may not
achieve much. Translate dreams into common
action. Much good can result from this.*

Doing Good

To do good always requires more than good intentions. It also requires good strategies that produce good results.

There are many men and women of goodwill in our community who actively seek to do good. Many of these people are not necessarily people with a religious faith. They may simply hold values that reflect concern for the improvement of society and the well-being of their neighbors.

It is to be hoped that this is also true of Christians. But more is required of them. Christians are called to do God's kind of good. So Ellul is right when he writes that "when we say that man can't do good on his own, it means that man can't do God's will without God."[2] For Christians see good primarily as doing the will of God.

This kind of good involves more than social upliftment. It means coming to enjoy God's shalom; entering His kingdom of peace, righteousness, and justice; and loving our neighbor as ourselves.

Reflection
*God's kind of good always involves
transformation based on
the grace of God.*

Embracing the Future

*While we need to appreciate the past and
realistically face the present, it is the future
that beckons us.*

Prayer will always be difficult for us in our pragmatic
age. In fact, it is often seen as escapism. It is
regarded as the practice of those who can no longer
responsibly take life into their own hands.

However, prayer can be the opposite of escapism.
It can be a straining toward a better future. Ellul
remarks that "to pray is to carry oneself toward the
future."[3] This is not because one can't face the present, but because one believes that the God who is
ahead of us is calling us into new possibilities. New
ways of thinking. The creation of new communities.
New ways of acting. Better ways of serving. New forms
of leadership. Greater participatory processes.

The person who prays, therefore, may well be laying the foundations for a better world.

Reflection
*Prayer is always the starting point
for new activities that seek to
achieve God's good in our world.*

Example

We have so dichotomized life that we foolishly think that we should heed a person's message without noting his or her lifestyle.

Life cannot be split up so easily. How we live reflects our beliefs and our beliefs manifest themselves in a particular lifestyle. It is imperative that, in learning from others, we also take note of how they live. Ellul comments: "Look at the one speaking. . . . Learn that person's life, and then take his or her words seriously or don't."[4]

If this is to occur, then many preachers will have to come down from their ivory towers and make themselves more accessible and vulnerable. Here Christian community becomes a viable option, because it is in the sharing together of life that one can more adequately know the other and learn from seeing and not from hearing only.

Action
Teach by modeling. This is an important corollary to preaching.

The Kingdom of God

*While church and kingdom are related, the
former is always subordinate to the latter and
the kingdom is the more comprehensive reality.*

The kingdom is God's action in the world. And this
action was made most clearly visible in the person and work of Jesus Christ. Therefore, the kingdom
is present wherever the words and ways of Jesus are
proclaimed and embodied.

Yet the presence of the kingdom is not under our
control. It cannot be reduced to mere institutional reality. The kingdom is not a system. It is the rule and reign
of God. It is a dynamic, not an organization. It is a power
rather than a structure. The kingdom appears where
God's will is done through the power of the Spirit. It is
there where God's shalom is present and where God's
peace, mercy, and justice are made manifest.

Reflection
*The kingdom of God, Jacques Ellul writes,
"is not the report of an observable,
measurable reality . . . it is an
affirmation of a counter-reality."*[5]

Commitment

*Committing ourselves to doing the will of God
does not mean that we meet God's demands
through our own resources.*

There are two extremes in the Christian life. The one
is passivity, where we expect God to do everything.
The other is an activism where we work as if everything only depended on us. Both extremes should be
avoided.

Ellul points out that "God does everything and
you must do everything."[6] God is wholly committed
to us as the covenant-keeping God. We need to be
wholly committed to Him as a people marked by faithfulness and obedience. God guides; we need to obey.
God empowers; we need to serve. God gives us talents
and gifts; we need to use them for His glory.

In fact, if we don't use what God has given us, we
will surely impoverish our own lives.

Reflection
*The Bible states: To whom much
is given, much is required.*

Escape

In this life there is no final "No." There is always the possibility of God's radical intervention and transformation.

We are far more likely to give up on people than God is. His is an all-pursuing love. Ours is often far more faltering. Yet, in spite of all appearances to the contrary, there can be no final word on even the "worst" of people. The labels of "insane," "criminal," "deviant," "pervert" do not ultimately imprison people.

Ellul comments: "We can escape destiny. . . . The worst man, the most lost, is not lost."[7] There is always the possibility in Christ to break the bonds that bind us. I have seen many "hopeless" people wonderfully converted. And they have frequently manifested a far greater passion for the kingdom of God than the conversion of "nice" people. In this life, our No is countermanded by God's Yes.

Reflection
God's grace is endless.

Lifestyle

Sadly, Christians in the West are known more for what they believe than for a distinctive lifestyle.

So much of life has become dichotomized. We have separated theory and practice, faith and life. But the pressing question for the Christian is not only "What must I believe?" but also "How should I live?"

Clearly, these two questions are intimately related. Ellul writes that the type of life for Christians "includes the way we think about present political questions as well as our way of practising hospitality."[8] In other words, it is a lifestyle that involves the social as well as the personal dimensions of life.

While the risk in spelling out guidelines is legalism, avoidance may well lead to a docetic Christianity where the social dimensions of our faith remain underdeveloped.

Reflection
The way we live will either verify the power of the gospel or bring it into disrepute.

To Call into Question

The power of the question lies in its ability to see other possibilities.

Some people take a passive approach to life. This may be part of their culture, where things are accepted rather than questioned. Others take a more questioning approach. This should be encouraged rather than suppressed. Ellul comments that "the movement toward freedom leads the individual to call into question . . . the external constraints by the group."[9]

While social reality is premised upon structures and institutions and we all need to live within certain constraints, this never means that we should simply accept things the way they are. Change is always necessary lest things stagnate. Therefore, the power of the question lies in its ability to move us beyond the present into new ways of being and acting.

Reflection
*The asking of good questions is
more difficult than giving
right answers.*

Unpredictable?

In our careful theologizing, we have reduced the God of this universe to a static formula rather than celebrating His majesty and glory.

While the God who acts in human history is consistent with the self-revelation of His being in Scripture, God cannot be bound. He defies our categories. He is neither male nor female. He is both glorious and humble in Jesus Christ. He is visible in Christ and mysterious as the Spirit.

As such, we cannot readily predict what God will do. He both judges and forgives. He is long-suffering, but not endlessly. He builds up, but also pulls down. Ellul notes that "God has always the full and perfect freedom to act in this surprising and disruptive fashion."[10]

God knows nothing about our schedules and priorities; at least He takes no note of them. He has His own agenda and acts accordingly. While God is attentive to the cry of the humble, He acts according to His own sovereignty and power.

Action
God is wholly other.
Worship Him as such.

For Others

*There is nothing so sterile as a Christianity
that seeks to benefit only its own.*

Jesus has rightly been described as the Man for others. While He lived for the sake of the kingdom of God, this kingdom was to benefit all. It meant reconciliation for the alienated. Forgiveness for the sinner. Empowerment for the poor. Hope for the disillusioned. And, finally, the transformation of the whole world.

We are also to live for the kingdom and this means that we will seek to benefit others. As Ellul points out: "We are liberated, not to make ourselves happy, but to live effectively, to be in the world, to go everywhere bearing liberty."[11] This is a challenge, a privilege, and a way of life. To live for others will always challenge our selfishness.

This cannot come by way of law, but only by grace, and therefore will always be an act of worship and thankfulness. And such a way of life will have to be intrinsic to who we are. We cannot turn it off and on. It will need to reflect our very being.

Reflection
*To be for others is not to work
against yourself. It is expressing
what God has meant us to be.*

Freedom

Only freedom frees us for true responsibility.

Ellul points out that "it is not true that people want to be free. They want the advantages of independence without the duties or difficulties of freedom."[12] Freedom not only unshackles us from the old; it more importantly opens us to new possibilities. While the release from the old has a euphoric quality, the grasping of new possibilities is the responsible face of freedom. Here it is no longer a matter of beating the drum of what we do not want, but a careful fashioning of what we do want.

This calls for a much greater effort on our part, for if we can envision and shape the new, then we are the makers of history rather than the victims of inevitable historical forces. If this is possible, then we also have to live with the consequences of what we create. Then, neither God nor chance is to blame when things don't turn out the way we expected. We only have ourselves to blame and need the courage to start again.

Reflection
*The consequence of freedom is
that we have to own much
more of what happens.*

Repentance

The most powerful impulse for the ethical life is neither the Law, which directs but does not empower, nor grace, which frees yet can so easily make us self-indulgent, but repentance, which catapults us into a new way of living.

Ellul reminds us that "only faith and repentance can give at one and the same time both the patience to endure and also the courage to fight."[13] For in enduring the difficulties of life, repentance frees us from the very present threat to blame, feel sorry for ourselves, or become bitter and harping.

In escaping these death-dealing attitudes that sap our strength and banish our hopes, we are freed for more positive responses. Repentance opens the door for creativity. It clears a pathway for God to act. It invites the presence of the Holy Spirit. It opens the way for the kingdom of God to be manifest. Repentance is not a morbid groveling that leaves us passive and defeated. It instead empowers us to grasp the new.

Reflection
Repentance leads not only to the joy-filled life, but to a life of reconstruction.

God's Enabling

While we can achieve so much by virtue of our human creativity and ability, God's benediction will make a significant difference.

This is not at all to suggest that God simply adds to what we do. It is not a matter of us making something beautiful and God adding some extra color. Nor is it a matter of doing good and God making it better. This is not what is meant when Ellul writes: "All human action is only effective if it is filled with the fullness that God gives it."[14]

God's participation changes things rather than merely adding to them. God often changes our priorities. He reminds us of the one thing needful that should be done now. He challenges us about the means that we use. Where we might be coercive, He challenges us to servant leadership. God will always impress upon us His kingdom values where the poor are rich and the way of power is through reconciliation.

Reflection
God sometimes takes away. Sometimes, He fills our empty hands. At other times, He completely redirects our priorities and our agendas.

Tradition

Tradition has the great benefit of providing a framework for security and continuity. But tradition as the carrier of the good is frequently the enemy of the best.

Without tradition, life would be very difficult, if not impossible. In the West, we stand in a long intellectual tradition going back to ancient Greek philosophy. The East has its own traditions. The church also has a long history and we neglect its richness to our peril. But tradition should serve the present—it should not usurp the future.

Thus tradition should be creatively utilized for future possibilities. It cannot remain static. Tradition must dialectically respond to the present. This usually means that not all of the tradition is retained. Nor is all of it rejected. This process of retention and rejection implies that we will move forward. Ellul is therefore right that "we should not seek to turn the clock back either individually or collectively."[15] Such turning back gives tradition a power it does not deserve, for that would bind both human creativity and the ongoing action of God in our world.

Reflection

Those who are afraid of the future cling to past traditions. Those who anticipate the future use the past as a starting point for the new.

The Love of God

*The world is graced by the love of God. Both
His general love for the world and His specific
love for people is everywhere manifest.*

While we may readily think that this world is
dominated by hate, violence, and despair, the
opposite is, in fact, true. Even in the urban slums of
the Third World, one finds hope, community, and solidarity. And in the centers of power where corruption
and exploitation are often rampant, there are men and
women of goodwill who have dedicated their lives to
the common good.

Sadly, evil in our world receives so much attention,
while the good is often unnoticed. Yet everywhere,
women and men are marked by God's grace and so
reflect something of God's love. Ellul is therefore right
in his confession that "in Jesus Christ we have received
the irrevocable certainty that, no matter what happens,
God loves all of us more than we can ever know."[16]

Reflection
*It is love rather than hate that is
the pervasive power in the universe.*

The Problem of Objectification

*The heart of Christianity is a personal
encounter with the living God. But we have
frequently made it belief in a set of dogmas
and participation in religious ceremonies.*

The problem with us is that we want to remake what
God has so wonderfully done. We want to reshape
the world instead of carefully guarding and using it. We
also attempt to reshape God's redemptive activity. We
turn revelation into dogma. Grace into law. Community
into institution. And we make God's freedom into a predictable certainty.

This human movement from charisma to rou-
tinization reflects our desire for permanence and for
control. We are afraid to live in God's presence and so
we dwell in the midst of religious ceremonies.
Moreover, because we want certainty, we create the
very structures that make life safe and predictable, but
closed off to the transcendent.

Reflection

*Ellul writes: "People invariably succeed in
gaining control of the contents of revelation . . .
they objectify it, transform a momentary
illumination into a permanent
establishment, a promise into a law, hope into
an institution, [and] love into a series
of works and charities."*[17]

A Religious World?

Religion is alive and well in the modern world.
The problem is that we have changed our gods.

Many sociologists of religion and many theologians have waxed eloquent about the secularization of the Western world. They have noted that many churches are virtually empty and that Christianity is less of a force in political and social life, in marked contrast to what is happening in many Third World countries where Christianity is virile and expanding.

But other scholars, including Jacques Ellul, have noted that "the modern world is above all else a religious world."[18] This assessment is correct. The West is not antireligious. It has simply changed its gods. Rejecting a sterile Christianity, men and women turned elsewhere for meaning and hope. There is a profound quest for spirituality and the making of a better and gentler world. If Christianity in the West is to regain a foothold, it must first of all learn to drink at the fountain of its own heritage and reclaim the vision from which it originally sprang.

Reflection

Only a Jesus faith reflected in a Jesus lifestyle
will cause men and women to think again
about the claims of Christianity.

Social Inequality

*In a world with such copious resources, the
problem of poverty is one of morality and not
simply one of economics.*

Ellul asserts that "the unbalanced distribution of
wealth and power are absolutely intolerable."[19] This
ideal of power-sharing remains an illusory reality in
our pragmatic world. While the economic conditions
of the middle classes have improved in the last fifty
years, the condition of the world's poor remains
much the same, despite all the efforts of aid and development programs.

Not only do many countries function under a ruling elite; the church also fails in the art of power
sharing. The vision of an egalitarian brotherhood and
sisterhood remains a vague though dangerous memory in the church's tradition. However, the church can
hardly raise its voice in seeking a more just social order
unless it begins to demonstrate a lifestyle based on
sharing and justice.

Action
*Build a just community. This task
is the greatest challenge facing
the contemporary church.*

Rest

*The blessing of rest can only follow the joy and
challenge of meaningful work.*

Meaningful work is becoming a rare commodity in
our modern world. In the Third World, people
are still subject to wearisome toil. In the First World,
meaningful work also eludes us due to increasing technology and the shrinking labor market.

Yet work remains important to us. It defines our
social identity and expresses our giftedness and abilities. It is when work is well done that rest becomes
a joyful reality. Ellul comments that "rest is not bore-
dom or satiation. It is the discovery of love finally
achieved and realised."[20] Rest, in other words, is not
doing nothing. Rest involves celebration. It is a sense
of well-being. Rest is the culmination of work. Like
God, we need to rejoice over and reflect on the work
of our hands.

Reflection
*Rest is both the blessing that follows
our work and the preparation for
work that still needs to be done.*

Spiritual Warfare

*The heart of prayer is to see God's rule fully
established in the lives of people and in the
institutions of our land.*

Ellul comments: "If we remain obsessed with ourselves in prayer, we make it sterile. If . . . we are caught up in this warfare of the Lord, it works its own transformation."[21] This does not mean that spiritual warfare has nothing to do with our own needs and struggles. But spiritual warfare has much more to do with the prayer that seeks God's kingdom and seeks the banishment of satanic forces.

This kind of prayer will of necessity be an ongoing prayer, for neither the establishment of God's kingdom, nor the banishment of Satan will fully occur in our sin-scarred world. The blessings that flow from this kind of prayer are that God will open up cracks in previously impossible situations so that His light and love can generate new possibilities. And prayer for the kingdom will always enrich our own lives, for blessings are added to those who are kingdom seekers.

Action

*In faith, pray for the kingdom and for
the Devil's power to be vanquished.*

The Role of Women

*After many generations of suppression through
role stereotyping, women have now emerged as
equal partners to build a better world.*

While we need to be careful that we do not continue to promote the old stereotypes—men
shape the world, women mold the family; men are
aggressive and domineering, women are nurturing and
caring—it need not be a contribution to such stereotypes to acknowledge that the fuller participation of
women in mainstream society can contribute to the
building of a better world.

Ellul is even more positive. "I feel that women are
now far more capable than men of restoring a meaning to the world we live in."[22] My own experiences in
working with women in both secular employment and
in Christian ministry suggest that women have not
only contributed in terms of care, gentler processes,
and participatory practices, but also in terms of
insight, strength, power, and determination.

Reflection
*In the Creation mandate, both women
and men were given the task to rule
and shape God's world.*

Beyond Structures

While we need the structures of family, commu-
nity, and state, these should enhance people's
development and not suppress them.

Jacques Ellul is very careful in his statement: "We can
search the Scriptures to try to discover what reforms
are needed and how a temporary order of God can be
set up in the world on condition that we are aware of
its relative value."[23]

We can so easily fall into the trap of making simplistic crossovers from the biblical text to the modern
world and claim that this is a biblical view of marriage,
politics, community, the arts, and economics. And we
then set about imposing that on the rest of the world.

Many Christians seek to reinstitute a Christian
version of the Old Testament theocracy in the belief
that this will create a safer and better world. But the
biblical emphasis is more on living a particular quality of life of forgiveness and justice than on the creation
of structures.

Reflection
We need both changed individuals and
changed structures. But all need to
be open to further change.

Christian Community

*Church is not simply people under the Word of
God and participating in the sacraments.
Church is also people bound together in sharing
a common life in Christ.*

For many years, the Ellul family had a church in
their home. In this more natural setting, and following the pattern of the house churches in the New
Testament, they were able to express a more authentic way of being brothers and sisters together in Christ.
Moreover, they were able to overcome social barriers
in that some working-class families were an intimate
part of the fellowship.

When the people finally decided that they wanted
a church building and to become more institutionalized,
something of this spirit of solidarity was lost. In light
of this experience, Ellul remarks: "We are constantly
faced with the question of how to bring the church to
form a community."[24] The church is never simply an
institution. It is people in relationship in Christ.

Reflection
*Community is essentially a different
form of social order than institution.*

Holy Spirit

Life devoid of the power of the Spirit can only in the end be sterile. Life in the Spirit can be significant, creative, and fruitful.

The Holy Spirit is the gentle member of the Godhead. Unobtrusive, yet significant. Peaceful, yet powerful. The Spirit is the servant member of the Godhead, making real in our lives the work of Christ and working in the world in creative and caring ways.

The Spirit is the go-between. The Spirit is the beautifier. The Spirit is the great community builder as we see in the early chapters of the book of Acts. As illusive as the wind. As purifying as fire. As gentle as a dove. As healing as oil.

The Spirit convicts of sin and showers God's people with talents and gifts. The Spirit illumines our minds and guides our footsteps. Life without the Spirit is a closing of the door to God's greatest gift. To have the Spirit possess us is great empowerment.

Reflection

The Holy Spirit, Ellul writes, "makes the work of Jesus Christ actual and living."[25]

Trendy

*There are two extremes. The one is to be so
preoccupied with the past as to be irrelevant.
The other is to be so contemporary that one
swallows whatever is the latest trend.*

Christians are frequently typified as reactionaries.
They are seen as living in the past with outmoded
values and ideas. Other Christians are quite the opposite. They are contemporary and trendy. Ellul is
concerned about both, but in writing about the latter
he states: "What troubles me is that Christians conform to the trend of the moment without introducing
into it anything specifically Christian."[26]

The challenge for Christians is to be relevant
rather than reactionary or trendy. The point is not to
resist change or simply to go along with whatever is
happening. Instead, Christians are called to shape the
world in harmony with the values of the kingdom of
God. As such, Christians need to be proactive in seeking to bring about change, but at the same time faithful
to the vision of Scripture.

Reflection
*The creative point is where old and new
meet to bring about something different.*

A Fragile World

In our beautiful world there is never an absence of difficulty and tragedy. Hence, there is always a call to exercise compassion.

There is a world of difference in the quality of life of the middle class of the First World and the poor of the Third World. The latter are undereducated, underemployed, undernourished, have a briefer life expectancy, and more readily experience the pain and difficulties of life.

Yet no matter who we are and where we live, we all experience something of life's fragility. None of us is without difficulty, disappointments, pain, faltering dreams, and faded hopes. We cannot insulate ourselves from life's imponderable realities. And bad things do happen to good people. If such be reality, it is imperative that we have the resources to face life. And such resources can only come, ultimately, from a deep-seated faith in the God who entered into the human fray.

Reflection

Ellul writes: "You cannot avoid bad and ruthless times crashing down on a person, not even with the best possible organisation of work and the economy."[27]

I and Thou

*In the intimate relationship of marriage, it is
important that the uniqueness and individuality
of each partner is fully respected.*

Marriage is a union. But this union is not the negation of individuality. Within the framework of a
common commitment, our uniqueness must be maintained. Ellul notes that "the period of recognition of
otherness is decisive." The one is not a reflection of the
other. The one is not made in the image of the other.
Each one made in God's image is different yet may experience complementarity.

Ellul goes on to write that once "differentness"
has been emphasized and is maintained, "the two
inseparables are safe within the equality of their
mutual love."[28] Marriage, therefore, is a wonderful
blend between self-affirmation and partnership, individuality and community, freeing and joining, and
uniqueness and collaboration. In the conjugal relationship, the "I" and "thou" are fully maintained and
only when this occurs does true complementarity exist.

Reflection
*While I need the other in marriage,
I also need to affirm myself.*

Discernment

Some people spiritualize everything. And while it may appear pious to attribute things to God, this may negate our own activity.

There are four factors that impact on our lives: what we do ourselves, the presence of God, the reality of evil spirits, and the forces of society. We need to learn to distinguish carefully which is which. It is all too easy to blame the Devil when we are the ones making the wrong choices. It is also possible that when we are congratulating ourselves, we should be praising God. Moreover, we may be blaming evil spiritual forces when in fact social factors are at play.

Discernment is therefore essential to the Christian life so that we are praising the right source and resisting the true Enemy. It is not effective to cast out the Devil when society's structures need to be changed. On the other hand, our ministry is hardly effective if we clothe people, but leave them demon-oppressed.

Reflection
"It is not God who makes my automobile speed up when I step on the accelerator,"[29] writes Ellul.

Teaching

Teaching is not simply the impartation of
knowledge. It is the honing of a mind.

While I have had a number of teachers who have
contributed to my spiritual, intellectual, and practical development, I have also adopted my own mentors.
Three more recent mentors have been Dietrich
Bonhoeffer, Henri Nouwen, and Jacques Ellul.

The major contribution that one's teachers or
mentors can make is not to provide answers, but to
stimulate us to ask further or new questions. Ellul,
speaking of his long teaching career and also his informal work, writes: "I found it extraordinary to transmit
something . . . to awaken a mind."[30]

The role of the teacher is to open up new horizons
and possibilities, not only to lay sound foundations. The
teacher's role is to see students both deeply rooted and
learning how to fly.

Reflection
To shape the mind is to begin to
shape the emerging new world.

DECEMBER

In the World

*If we are not actively seeking to change the
world, then the world is passively molding us.*

There is a rhythm to the Christian life. The most
basic is work and rest. A related rhythm is that of
contemplation and withdrawal on the one hand and
service and engagement on the other.

But while withdrawal can be for the purpose of
worship, reflection, and renewal, it should also be the
fuel for reengagement. This is necessary because we
have a profoundly important task in the world. We are
to continue to shape it and to utilize it responsibly. But
we are also called to work and pray to see God's kingdom made manifest in every facet of life.

Jacques Ellul, in developing particular training
programs, states: "We wanted each Christian layman
to become aware of his or her responsibility as a
Christian in society."[1] If the laity are not mobilized for
their role in the world, then the church's impact will
never amount to much.

Reflection

*The theological and ministry training
of the laity for their role in the world in
their normal occupations is a pressing
challenge for the church.*

Prayer and Responsibility

We cannot expect God to answer our prayers when He has already placed the means for the answer in our own hands.

In much of our praying, we are totally dependent on God to provide the answers. Because we cannot heal, only God can restore. Because we lack answers, only God can give us wisdom. Much of our praying, therefore, comes out of our vulnerability and need.

But there are prayers in which we need to play a part in providing the solution. As Ellul points out, "If God receives a prayer, the first consequence falls upon the praying person."[2] For example, we can hardly ask God to heal our inner conflicts and struggles if we are not prepared to deal with unforgiveness and bitterness, because the latter may be a significant contributor to our inner pain.

Action
The answers to some prayers lie in our own hands. Ask for God's grace to give us the courage to act.

God for Me

*While the being of God remains a mystery, I can
experience the presence of God as a strong
father and a caring mother.*

Ellul states it so simply: "I can tell only what God
has done for me, not who or what he is."[3] The theologians have tried to do much more. They have
attempted to explain the unexplainable. And so we
have become familiar with many terms: omnipresent,
immutable, unbegotten, and omnipotent.

While these and many other terms have their
usefulness, they hardly explain my experience of
God. We need to find very different words in an
attempt to articulate how God works in our lives. I
am awed by God. I experience His absence. I know
the reality of His forgiveness. I know He loves me and
cares for me. I experience His nearness. I know He
is guiding me. I know He is seeking to change things
in my life. While this sort of terminology may sound
awfully mundane, it has the ring of authenticity.

Reflection
*In God's action,
I know Him best.*

Contentment

*While contentment is an essential element of
happiness for those who already have much,
it is a virtue the poor can ill afford.*

Despite the emphasis on much-having in our
grossly materialistic age, the source of happiness
lies elsewhere. It certainly does not lie in the abun-
dance of possessions. Meaningful relationships and
work are far greater sources of happiness. So is the
experience of God's benediction on our lives. Ellul
writes: "Learn that God has approved of your life and,
on that basis, with your heart at peace, be happy with
the material things."[4]

All of this is good advice for those who already
have what they basically need. But this message is the
death knell for those who have not. Rather than contentment, they should be encouraged to struggle for
their own betterment. Their cry for justice should be
heard. And those who already have should join in partnership with the poor to alleviate their suffering.

Action
*Learn how to share and so
gain further contentment.*

Culture and Christianity

*Western culture is based more on a memory
of Christianity than on its reality.*

Western culture has developed many fine traditions and institutions. Most governments in the
West have implemented all sorts of welfare programs
for the needy and its laws protect the rights of the individual. Its technological progress has meant relative
security for everybody. There is much that we can be
thankful for.

But there is much that is flawed. Ellul asserts: "The
West is, in itself, the opposite of what God teaches and
bids us to live in Christ."[5] The West demonstrates a self-
sufficient arrogance. It is no longer a culture deeply
dependent on the grace and guidance of God. The West
reflects an individualism that no longer builds community. The West promotes ends over means and, in
its quest for progress and development, has left many
ethical questions unanswered. The West needs again
to be converted.

Reflection
*To the extent that the West neglects
its Christian roots, to that extent
it will fail to be truly great.*

Victims

There are those who are the victims of the
sins of others against them.

People not only sin. They are also sinned against.
We need only think of a bullying drunkard of a
husband and a timid, beaten wife. We can also think
of the victims of rape, incest, and emotional abuse, or
the victims of police corruption and dictatorial political regimes that are hell-bent on repressing dissent.
There are also the victims of racial discrimination,
social inequality, and economic exploitation.

In the midst of these depressing realities, Ellul can
assert that "God is not indifferent to the victims."[6] God
does heal the brokenhearted. He does fill the poor with
hope. He does give the victimized courage.

But all wrongs are not righted in this life.
Sometimes the wheels of justice turn all too slowly. In
the face of such realities, if bitterness and despair are
averted, then God has already drawn near.

Reflection
In the midst of injustice, the
flame of hope can burn brightly.

Solidarity

If Christians only extend spiritual comfort to each other, but do not demonstrate practical care, then the world will never catch a fuller glimpse of the kingdom of God.

It has been asserted that the problem is not that Christianity does not work, but that it has never been tried. This is an overt criticism of the lack of courage on the part of many Christians to live the radical demands of the gospel. But to assert that this has never been done is absurd. Throughout the church's long history, men and women have walked the road of a costly discipleship and built communities of love and solidarity. We need only think of the desert fathers, the Anabaptists, the Moravians, and of many Third World Christians today.

The pressing issue is whether the Christians of the West can follow the example of these brothers and sisters and their solidarity of faith expressed in basic Christian communities. Daring to do likewise may build a Christian renaissance in the West.

Reflection

Ellul reminds us that we need a "solidarity between Christians" that is "expressed in mutual help."[7]

Perseverance

If we have caught a vision of God's purposes in
the world, we can persevere against great odds.

There are no cheap victories in the Christian faith.
Hence, all the huffing and puffing of the "name-it-
and-claim-it" gospel is hopelessly off track. Christianity
had its beginnings in the suffering and death of Jesus
of Nazareth. It has a long history of martyrs. The
Christian faith, therefore, is much more one of perseverance than of conquests. Christians are the little flock
in a fallen world. They are called to a servant role and
are challenged to be salt and light in our troubled times.

Therefore, Christians are called to faithfulness and
perseverance no matter what happens. Ellul reminds
us that "we continue to act with maximum perseverance . . . in spite of the absence of temporal effect."[8]

Reflection
The act of perseverance can
only be an act of faith.

Inspiration

*Our hopes and dreams and our seemingly
strange intuitions are sometimes the precious
seed from which great things can develop.*

Our Christian religion knows the reality of propositional truth. It also knows the power of God acting decisively in history. But the Christian faith also knows the power of inspiration. Visions and dreams are part of the way in which God works.

Yet as Ellul rightly points out, "There is no inspiration . . . without discipline."[9] One can have dreams, but one needs to be more than just a dreamer. Dreams need to be discerned. They need to be operationalized in terms of specific strategies. And they need to be acted upon in the face of disbelief and opposition. Many a great idea has fallen on barren ground because there has not been the determination to follow it through.

Reflection
*Inspiration always needs to
join hands with practicality.*

The Word

The word may appear to be weaker than the deed, but the word directs the deed and explains it.

We all know from personal experience that words can be very powerful. Not only are consistent deeds of love important, but words of love are equally important. Conversely, negative words can have incredible power in our lives. Ellul reminds us that "when the word is not authentic, it is absolutely nothing."[10] The words "I love you" don't mean much if they are not meant and are not made practical.

Sadly, we are living in a world where the word has become deformed. So much is said with such passion, but we know that it lacks credibility. While this may be true of much political speak, it should never be true of religious speak, for Christianity is premised on the Word becoming deed, becoming flesh.

Reflection
*God's Word has become deed.
Our words should be likewise.*

Conformism

*In a world of technological uniformity, we need
to proclaim the freeing power of Christ, which
empowers people to radical nonconformity.*

Our modern world is characterized by uniformity.
This is occurring not only at the level of technology, but also at the level of culture. The church,
however, is called to be different. Not only are Christians
called to display a different set of values, but the church
itself should be characterized by diversity rather than
a uniform sameness.

Ellul writes: "I have never favored any sort of conformism or rigid unification."[11] In a world where the
specters of totalitarian systems still haunt us, the church
must never be the place of conformism. Instead, the
church should demonstrate unity in diversity.

Reflection
*Christ is the center point. He
brings people together. But He
also frees people to be themselves.*

The Seeking God

*God's grace is not simply exemplified in the
reality of forgiveness, but also in the fact that
God persistently seeks us out.*

There is a lot of emphasis in the contemporary
church on our seeking and finding God. While this
highlights our response of faith, this is putting the cart
before the horse. For it is much more a matter of God
seeking and finding us than the other way round.

God is like the hound of heaven. The persistent
lover. The One who goes out of His way to draw us to
Himself. He is already at work while we remain unaware.
He is already there even though we have failed to recognize Him. He gently, and sometimes more aggressively,
awakens us to a faith response where we joyfully bow
the knee to the One who loves us and made us for
Himself.

Reflection
*"Religion seeks to go from below, where we
are, to above, where God is. But the Bible
shows the opposite," writes Ellul.*[12]

The "Sameness" of People

People have always been faced with the possibility of greatness or desecration.

Ellul notes that "events change, as do conditions of life and standards of living, but people are basically the same."[13] This is only relatively true. We are hardly the same as our ancient forebears as far as living conditions, mental outlook, and world view.

In other ways, we are similar. Because all are made in God's image, all have the capacity to celebrate the good and eschew evil. We all have the need to find meaning for our lives. We all need to find forgiveness. We all need to use our talents and gifts. We all need to live authentically and resist the power of evil. And being such, we all have the need for God's grace in our lives.

But in each generation we need to be particularly discerning about how we can best serve God with relevance and power.

Reflection
While much has changed in the way we now live, we are still moral creatures needing to make important choices.

Upon Himself

*In Christ, God takes to Himself all of our
shame, guilt, and pain.*

The idea that God is vindictive and retaliatory is
nonsense. God is exactly the opposite. As Ellul
rightly points out: "God directs his justice upon himself; he has taken upon himself the condemnation of
our wickedness."[14] It is this that provides the basis for
our freedom and our joy. And it is this that provides
the foundation for our thankfulness and service. We,
the alienated ones, are welcomed home.

Little wonder that there is a dimension of ecstasy
in living the Christian life. We are miraculously set free
and can therefore serve our God in the world with glad
abandonment.

Reflection
*The heart of the gospel is not faith,
but the grace of God, which makes
the great reversal possible.*

Creativity

Creativity is not simply a gift. It is also the
result of a context that encourages questioning
and exploration.

Creativity is not only a gift of nature. It also has to
do with our social environment. Many people
lament that our social context restricts the development of creativity. And much of our schooling has not
helped us to think critically.

Ellul believes that "the most important thing is to
restore to man the maximum of his capacities of independence, invention and imagination."[15] We therefore
need to find new and possibly informal ways to empower
people for maximum learning.

The church in its programs should encourage creative learning for, after all, it celebrates the coming of
the Holy Spirit as the One who gives insight, leads us
into truth, and showers us with His gifts.

Action
Create contexts for
questioning and exploration.

Neighbor

*In all that we seek to do in the world, we
must not neglect building community with
our neighbor.*

Christians are rightly involved in all kinds of projects by which they seek to build a better world
based on peace and justice. In seeking to be salt and
light in the world, it is imperative that Christians are
not only committed to social activism, but also to celebration and worship.

Further, we need to find time to build community with our neighbor while we seek to do good in
our world. Ellul writes: "The most important thing that
we can do socially is to rediscover our neighbour."[16]
Our neighbor so easily slips from view in our busy
lives. Yet that neighbor is also the one who bears God's
image and needs that to be fully restored through the
grace of Christ.

Action
*Serve your neighbor and so reflect
something of the love of Christ.*

Everything

*God's redemptive work in Christ embraces
everything—my life, family, work, and the
whole created order.*

While we are to join with God in seeing His kingdom come to fuller realization, in one way we don't add anything to the kingdom. Its foundations are fully laid in Christ's redemptive work. Thus, we labor to see the kingdom unfold. We are not really the ones who are building the kingdom. Ellul puts it this way: "On this road it is not that half is done by God and half by man. The whole road has been made by God."[17]

God is the leader. We follow. God is the provider. We live out of His grace. God is building His kingdom. We are colaborers. God's Spirit is at work in the world. We join in the slipstream of the breath of God.

Action
*Walk in God's will; it is the
most telling place to be.*

Watchman

*To be a watchman in the house of God or in the
wider society is a role and task that should be
divinely given and not humanly sought.*

There is nothing glamorous about being a prophet
or a watchman. Prophets are seldom liked. They
are more frequently not heeded. They are often resisted. And they are generally rejected. Ellul saw himself
in precisely such a role. He writes: "I wanted to play
the role . . . of a watchman. But no-one listened to
me."[18] Ellul sought to be a watchman alerting people
to the consequences of technology in our age. In the
church, he sought to play a similar role by calling the
church to a greater authenticity and commitment to
the kingdom of God.

However, a prophet can finally not be concerned
about results, but only about faithfulness. And whether
the message is hard or easy, the prophet can only speak
with boldness and courage.

Reflection
*A prophet will always
walk a lonely road.*

Efficiency

*One of the driving forces in our modern world is
the desire for efficiency. While this is commend-
able in terms of production and progress, there is
a shadow side.*

Ellul notes that "what characterises technical action
within a particular activity is the search for greater
efficiency."[19] There is nothing wrong with seeking
greater efficiency. But there is everything wrong if efficiency becomes a value within itself and excludes other
considerations. When our drive for efficiency dehu-
manizes or marginalizes people, then efficiency
becomes demonic. Sadly, so much of the technological progress in our world lacks an appropriate ethic.

Here, those of us who are Christians have a role
to play. We are called to promote the values of the kingdom of God. These values include caring for the weak,
upholding justice, and doing good to all in a way that
reflects the way God treats us.

Consequently, we can never be committed to
progress for its own sake, but only to that which builds
a better world.

Reflection
*Our efficiency needs to be
matched with care and justice.*

No Limits

*Christ's redemptive work affects persons in
the totality of who they are and all of reality.*

There are no limits to the scope of Christ's redemptive work. God's grace affects us in body, soul, and spirit. And the Spirit's transformative work seeks to affect us in all that we are in all of our relationships and in all the contexts of our life.

God's redemptive work involves changing not only individuals, but also families, neighborhoods, and institutions. In fact, the whole of created reality will finally be made new in Christ. Ellul observes that "human beings are saved by Christ, but all that was thrust into disorder and rupture and incoherence is also saved."[20]

Hence, our task is not only one of evangelism, but also that of social concern and overcoming the results of structural evil. Christians, therefore, have a radical agenda. Our task is not so much to preserve the world, but to change it.

Action
*With God's help, do not simply wait for a new
heaven and a new earth, but build the new
world by the grace and power of God.*

Action

*There is little transformative power in
words without deeds.*

Most people regard Jacques Ellul as a Christian
intellectual. And he is that. He has written on
technology, violence, revolution, urbanism, politics,
ethics, theology, and the Bible. But there is another side
to Ellul. He writes: "I am by nature a man of action."[21]
He worked in the underground resistance during
World War II. He worked in local government politics. He worked to renew the church. He worked to
improve education. He worked with juvenile delin-
quents. He was involved with ecological issues. The
list could go on.

While Ellul himself admits that not all of his activities were successful, he believes that he would do them
again. For not to act is finally a sign of intellectual cow-
ardice. Belief mixed with passion makes no sense if it
doesn't lead to action. Careful research and analysis is
of little use unless new ways are attempted. Ellul, therefore, is a sign that the old dichotomy between theory
and practice can be overcome.

Reflection
*The world needs thinking
practitioners and thinkers who act.*

Propaganda

Every major institution has a way of legitimizing its role, task, and function in society. While something or much of the information transmitted by the institution may be accurate, some of it is pure propaganda.

Ellul points out that "a modern state . . . must use propaganda as a means of governing."[22] In our everyday lives, we experience the impact of such propaganda. Information is structured in such a way that it favors the state. Those who govern are thereby made to look more credible. While some accept this without question, most citizens can see this for what it is.

The use of propaganda should not characterize the church, however. The proclamation of the truth of the gospel should be done with integrity. When the church speaks about its life, ministry, and impact, it should do so with integrity. It must resist resorting to propaganda in order to make itself more attractive and acceptable. After all, the church consists of broken people who have received a measure of God's grace and beggars who have received food.

Reflection

Propaganda masks the truth, but we are called to display the truth in all we do.

Ability

*Ability is a careful blend of giftedness and
training.*

Ability can be innate. But it also has to do with careful honing and development. To be a person of ability means that one has concentrated on developing certain skills and aspects of oneself.

While this is good in that it reflects an ability to focus and particularize, there is also a down side. As Ellul points out, "You must know your ability and its limitations."[23] Or, to put that somewhat differently, every development of certain skills means a lack of equal opportunity to develop other skills. This means that we cannot equally develop other aspects of who we are.

As a result, we are not all-rounders and wholeness remains an illusive quest. Therefore, we will have to learn to live with limitations, even those that could have been developed into strengths. Thus, even in the midst of our abilities, we need to acknowledge our creaturely limitations.

Reflection
*In strenuously becoming one thing,
we are forced to deny other parts of
who we are and who we could be.*

Answers

*In a world marred by sin and with structures of
oppression, there are answers. But they never
will be as complete as we would like them to be.*

In the face of injustice and oppression and the persistent human predicament of wandering from the sheltering presence of God who alone can meaningfully shape and direct our lives, God has unleashed His redemptive power. And it is this power flowing from His grace that can make the difference in our lives and in our world. As a result, there are answers. Ellul reminds us that "God makes it possible for us to come up with an answer and discover the way out."[24]

This does not mean that the answers will be complete. Nor does it mean that we do nothing and simply wait for God to act. Rather, it means that with God's help we forge strategies for hope and renewal. But these strategies will only work when they are founded not only on the wisdom of God, but also on the power of God.

Reflection
*While we can readily come up with our
own answers, we need answers born
out of the wisdom of God.*

God with Us

The miracle is that God joins us in the midst of life. He neither remains aloof nor unconcerned.

At this time of the year, we celebrate the wonder of the Incarnation. In the words of Ellul, God "leaves his peaceful heaven and takes upon himself all that man undergoes."[25] In ages past also, God drew near. He heard the cry of His people in their Egyptian captivity and delivered them in the Exodus event.

But in Christ, God draws near in a more significant way. His is the drawing near of identification. This is no longer the God of power delivering His people by awesome acts. It is the God of weakness demonstrating that the way of the Cross, the way of suffering, is the greatest transformative power in the world. In Christ, our sins are forgiven and our weakness turned into strength.

Reflection
*In the Incarnation, we not only have
a redemptive process, but a model for
a new way of working in the world.*

A Prophetic Voice

*Believing in the final establishment of God's new
heaven and new earth should not move us to
earthly unconcern. Instead, it should move us to
anticipate the end in our present existence.*

Ellul makes a seemingly contradictory statement.
"Every Christian . . . is now a prophet of the
return of Christ and by this very fact he has a revolutionary mission in politics."[26] Some Christians believe
that these two ideas are mutually exclusive. Longing
for the return of Christ means that a person withdraws
from the world of politics, the arts, or economics.

But the opposite should be the case. Longing for
a new heaven and a new earth calls us to worldly
engagement. For love and justice call us to make present the future. One cannot see the final good without
having the moral responsibility to make that visible
now. One cannot believe for something better and
remain immobilized. The vision of the future calls us
to worldly responsibility.

Reflection
*Only a moral coward longs for
the new and fails to attempt it.*

Structure and Creativity

*We need structures and institutions. We also
need to curb their powers and make them
responsive to human needs.*

Ellul, in describing his life's work states: "I am plead-
ing for the regression of all the powers of order."[27]
This is not to say that structures and institutions are
not important. God is the God of order who has reg-
ulated the importance of family, state, work, and
church.

But structures and institutions can also become
oppressive and serve their own ends. The state is not
an end in itself. It is meant to do God's good in the
world and to serve those to whom it is accountable. The
tragedy in our modern world has been the devolution
of the role and responsibilities of individuals and the
increase in the powers of experts and institutions. In
this way, we have become more infantile rather than
coming of age.

We need to work for people power and this must
start in the church, where members assume responsibility for expressing their life together in Christ.

Action
*Encourage people to take responsibility
rather than become dependent.*

Against the Tide

Christians are called to live by the divine
contrariness of Jesus who did not join the
religious establishment, or the world-denying
Essenes, or the politically radical Zealots.

Jesus' agenda was the kingdom of God. This kingdom was a spiritual reality in the hearts and lives
of people. It was also a social reality. It has to do with
new relationships built on love and reconciliation, and
new economic realities based on sharing and care for
the poor.

In following in the footsteps of Jesus, we too are
to live a different set of values than those promoted
by the world. We are called to resist the powers of this
age. Ellul reminds us that "to affirm a transcendent
over against technique is the way of nonconformity
today."[28] Order, technique, methods, and programs
should not absorb us to the detriment of relationships
that are built on love and justice and empower people
to live in the light of God's kingdom.

Reflection
The church should be more a caring
community than an institution.

True Happiness

Happiness cannot come from a life of make-believe, but only from a life of integrity.

Happiness is always a byproduct. Those who seek it directly will probably never find it. Happiness is the fruit that we enjoy when we live in faithfulness and with integrity. Even in the midst of difficulty and pain, happiness can well up as refreshing water.

Ellul, however, underscores this with a note of realism. He writes: "We must not hope that tomorrow will be much better, so that we try at all costs to fabricate some unexpected perfect happiness."[29] Happiness does not come from idealization. Nor is it the product of escapism. We cannot even manipulate the conditions for happiness.

True happiness is a gift. It comes on the heels of faithfulness, perseverance, and obedience to the ways of God.

Action
Seek to please God and serve your neighbor, and happiness will be the surprising bonus that will make your life full.

Faith

*Faith acknowledges the way God has acted in
the past and tenaciously holds Him to act in
similar ways today.*

Ellul insists that "faith is not a place of refuge for
passive souls; it implies the will to change the
world."[30] Faith does not know the language of security. It only knows the language of risk and courage.
For faith is centered in the God who acts in history to
bring about righteousness and justice.

Faith is not centered in faith. Faith ought not to
be centered in much of the world-denying pietistic
preaching of our contemporary pulpits. Faith should
not be based on our own anemic version of the gospel.
Rather, it should be based on the God of the Exodus,
the God of the prophets, and the God of our Lord Jesus
Christ who came to set captives free.

God has never revealed Himself as quietistic or
passive, but as the God who acts. Faith then links us
to such a God and such a program.

Reflection
*Faith is not escapism, but worldly
engagement in the light of heavenly realities.*

The Power of This Age

Christ has shown where true power lies. It lies in servanthood, not in manipulation or oppression.

Christ exposed the moral bankruptcy of a tired and legalistic Judaism that crucified its prophets. He discredited Roman rationality and justice when it accepted the robber rather than the innocent. Christ's light has a way of penetrating and exposing other ideologies and systems that, while they hold such promises for good, turn out to be empty cisterns that hold no refreshment. Ellul reminds us that "it is the certainty of faith . . . that, through the crucifixion of Jesus Christ, the powers of this world have been conquered."[31]

In contrast to our systems, Christ has paved a different way. Reconciliation rather than enmity. Justice rather than exploitation. Peace rather than aggression. Servanthood rather than power. Grace rather than legalism. Community rather than individualism. In living out such a vision, the powers of this age will be vanquished in the victory of Christ.

Action
Dare to resist. Dare to oppose. Dare to walk the new way. And dare to build the new.

1912   Born on January 6 in Bordeaux, France.
        His father was a Serbian aristocrat and his
        mother French. His mother, but not his
        father, was a Christian. He was an only
        child.

1928   Attended the University of Bordeaux.

1929   His parents lost everything in the financial
        crash of 1929. As a result, Jacques Ellul
        could say, "I experienced true poverty in
        every way."

1930   Avidly read Karl Marx's *Das Kapital*. This
        helped Ellul to understand his family's
        poverty and struggle.

1932   Became a Christian. Ellul wrote: "It was a
        very brutal and very sudden conversion."
        Eventually, he became a Protestant and
        joined the Reformed Church. He came
        under the influence of Karl Barth's theology.

1933   Became involved politically in a French
        antifascist movement.

1934–37 Though he made contact with both social-
        ists and communists but never joined them,
        he completely broke with communism dur-
        ing the Moscow trials, which demonstrated
        that communism had become a totalitarian
        system. Yet the influence of Marx remained
        important in that it "instilled a revolution-
        ary tendency in me," emphasized the
        "importance of reality" and helped shape
        "my decision to side with the poor."

1937	Married Yvette Lensvelt.
1937	Defended his doctoral thesis in the Faculty of Law at the University of Bordeaux on the ancient Roman institution called the *Mancipium*.
1937–39	Lectured in the Faculty of Law at the University of Bordeaux. Also lectured at the University of Montpellier and the University of Strasbourg.
1940	Was dismissed from his part-time university post at Strasbourg for his opposition to Marshall Petain and the Vichy government.
1942	Joined the French underground resistance movement to German military occupation.
1944–46	Deputy mayor of Bordeaux in charge of public works.
1944–47	Secretary of the Movement of National Liberation in France, which sought to achieve more radical changes in society.
1944–80	Professor of the History and Sociology of Institutions in the Faculty of Law and Economic Sciences at the University of Bordeaux.
1947–51	Served on study commissions of the World Council of Churches.
1951–70	A member of the National Council of the Reformed Church in France.
1947–80	Professor of social history at the Institute of Political Studies at Bordeaux.
1958–76	Worked with juvenile delinquents.
1965	Received *Docteur Honoris Causa* from the Free University of Amsterdam.
1968–	Worked on nuclear and ecological issues and the national planning of land use.

1980–94	Retired from the University of Bordeaux and the Institute of Political Studies and continued his prolific writing until his death.
1994	Died May 19, 1994.

ENDNOTES

Jᴀɴᴜᴀʀʏ

1. *What I Believe*, p. 1
2. *The Judgment of Jonah*, p. 49
3. *Living Faith: Belief and Doubt in a Perilous World*, p. 71
4. *The Betrayal of the West*, p. 16
5. *Jesus and Marx: From Gospel to Ideology*, p. 2
6. *Propaganda: The Formation of Men's Attitudes*, p. xvi
7. *Living Faith: Belief and Doubt in a Perilous World*, p. xxviii
8. *Money & Power*, p. 19
9. *What I Believe*, p. 16
10. *The Politics of God and the Politics of Man*, pp. 61-62
11. *The Judgment of Jonah*, p. 85
12. *Jesus and Marx: From Gospel to Ideology*, p. 7
13. *Living Faith: Belief and Doubt in a Perilous World*, p. 62
14. *Money & Power*, p. 27
15. *The Ethics of Freedom*, p. 271
16. *What I Believe*, p. 54
17. *The Betrayal of the West*, p. 8
18. *The Judgment of Jonah*, p. 89
19. *The Politics of God and the Politics of Man*, p. 58
20. *Living Faith: Belief and Doubt in a Perilous World*, p. 29
21. *Jesus and Marx: From Gospel to Ideology*, p. 5
22. *Money & Power*, p. 18
23. *The Ethics of Freedom*, pp. 276-277
24. *What I Believe*, p. 37
25. *The New Demons*, p. 212
26. *The Judgment of Jonah*, p. 84
27. *The Politics of God and the Politics of Man*, p. 69
28. *Hope in Time of Abandonment*, p. 259
29. *Living Faith: Belief and Doubt in a Perilous World*, p. 22
30. *Jesus and Marx: From Gospel to Ideology*, p. 6
31. *Money & Power*, p. 19

April

JUNE

SEPTEMBER

OCTOBER

November

BIBLIOGRAPHY OF JACQUES ELLUL'S WRITINGS

The Theological Foundation of Law, Marguerite Wieser (trans.), SCM, 1960.

The Technological Society, John Wilkenson (trans.), Vintage Books, 1964.

The Presence of the Kingdom, Olive Wyon (trans.), Seabury, 1967.

The Political Illusion, Konrad Keller (trans.), Alfred A. Knopf, 1967.

A Critique of the New Commonplaces, Helen Weaver (trans.), Alfred A. Knopf, 1968.

Violence: Reflections from a Christian Perspective, Cecelia Gaul Kings (trans.), Seabury, 1969.

To Will and To Do, C. Edward Hopkin (trans.), Pilgrim, 1969.

The Meaning of the City, Dennis Pardee (trans.), Eerdmans, 1970.

The Judgment of Jonah, Geoffrey W. Bromiley (trans.), Eerdmans, 1971.

Autopsy of Revolution, Patricia Wolf (trans.), Alfred A. Knopf, 1971.

The Politics of God and the Politics of Man, Geoffrey W. Bromiley (trans.), Eerdmans, 1972.

False Presence of the Kingdom, C. Edward Hopkin (trans.), Seabury, 1972.

Propaganda: The Formation of Men's Attitudes, Konrad Keller and Jean Lerner (trans.), Random House, 1973.

Hope in Time of Abandonment, C. Edward Hopkin (trans.), Seabury, 1973.

Prayer and Modern Man, C. Edward Hopkin (trans.), Seabury, 1973.

The New Demons, C. Edward Hopkin (trans.), Seabury, 1975.

The Ethics of Freedom, Geoffrey W. Bromiley (trans. and ed.), Eerdmans, 1976.

Apocalypse: The Book of Revelation, George W. Schreiner (trans.), Seabury, 1977.

The Betrayal of the West, Matthew J. O'Connell (trans.), Seabury, 1978.

Perspectives on Our Age: Jacques Ellul Speaks on His Life and Work, William. H. Vanderburg (ed.) and Joachim Neugroschel (trans.), Seabury, 1981.

In Season, Out of Season: An Introduction to the Thought of Jacques Ellul (based on interviews by Madeleine Garrigou-Lagrange), Harper & Row, 1982.

Living Faith: Belief and Doubt in a Perilous World, Peter Heinegg (trans.), Harper & Row, 1983.

Money & Power, La Vonne Neff (trans.), InterVarsity, 1984.

The Humiliation of the Word, Joyce Main Hanks (trans.), Eerdmans, 1985.

The Subversion of Christianity, Geoffrey W. Bromiley (trans.), Eerdmans, 1986.

Jesus and Marx: From Gospel to Ideology, Joyce Main Hanks (trans.), Eerdmans, 1988.

What I Believe, Geoffrey W. Bromiley (trans.), Eerdmans, 1989.

The Technological Bluff, Geoffrey W. Bromiley (trans.), Eerdmans, 1990.

Reason For Being: A Meditation on Ecclesiastes, Joyce Main Hanks (trans.), Eerdmans, 1990.

About the Author

CHARLES RINGMA is an Australian trained at Reformed Theological College in Victoria. He holds degrees in divinity, sociology, and studies in religion. He has a Ph.D. in philosophical hermeneutics from the University of Queensland. He has served as a community worker among the Aborigines as well as the poor in Manila, and was professor of theology and missions at the Asian Theological Seminary. He established Teen Challenge in Australia. He is presently professor of missions and evangelism at Regent College, Vancouver.

MOVE CLOSER TO CHRIST WITH THESE MEDITATIVE RESOURCES.

Seize the Day

Does your faith live inside church walls? This compilation of Dietrich Bonhoeffer's writings offers a look at the meaning of life and Christ in the world beyond church doors. Challenge yourself to move from the safety of the sanctuary into a troubled world that desperately needs the love of a savior.

Seize the Day (Charles Ringma) $10

Dare to Journey

Change begins on the inside. But our busy lives leave us with few resources to power even the mildest of inner revolutions. Charles Ringma's meditative reader, written as a set of conversations with Henri Nouwen, will empower you to re-engage yourself in the tasks of life with new fervor and hope.

Dare to Journey (Charles Ringma) $10

Get your copies today at your local bookstore, visit our website at www.navpress.com, or call (800) 366-7788 and ask for offer **#6095** or a FREE catalog of NavPress products.

NAVPRESS
BRINGING TRUTH TO LIFE
www.navpress.com

Prices subject to change.